BORN DIFFERENT

BORN DIFFERENT

DIFFERENT

Amazing Stories of Very Special People

FREDERICK DRIMMER

ATHENEUM   1988   New York

Picture credits: pages 2, 31, 41, 46, 102, 103, Bridgeport Public Library; pages 9, 48, 59, 64, 67, 69, Alton *Telegraph*; page 72, Royal College of Surgeons of England; page 119, Southern Historical Collection, University of North Carolina; pages 126, 129, 137, 142, 145, 148, London Hospital Medical College Museum.

Atheneum, Macmillan Publishing Company, 866 Third Avenue, New York, NY 10022
Collier Macmillan Canada, Inc.
First Edition   Printed in U.S.A.   10   9   8   7   6   5   4   3   2   1   ·

Library of Congress Cataloging-in-Publication Data
Drimmer, Frederick.   Born different: amazing stories of very special people
Bibliography: p.   Includes index.   1. Abnormalities, Human—Biography—Juvenile Literature. I. Title.
QM691.D75   1988   920   [B]   87-33354   ISBN 0-689-31360-8

*The world breaks everyone
and afterward many are strong at the broken places.*

Ernest Hemingway

Contents

Acknowledgments

For such a short book I am astonished to see how long is the list of people and institutions whose advice, help, and encouragement I found indispensable while I was planning and writing it.

To Marcia Marshall, my editor, I am greatly indebted for her interest in this project and for her sensitive and warm support, helping me carry it from idea to reality.

Dr. David Rimoin, M.D., Ph.D., director of the department of pediatrics and of the Medical Genetics–Birth Defect Center of Cedar–Sinai Medical Center, Los Angeles, California, provided expert information about dwarfism as well as illuminating criticism of my preliminary pages on the subject. Harriet Stickney, information coordinator of Little People of America, Inc., San Bruno, California, brought me up to date on the activities of her fine organization.

Dee Quinn, genetics counselor of the University of Connecticut, and the directors of the March of Dimes furnished important facts about congenital malformations.

For sharing his special knowledge and judicious insights about Julia Pastrana—covering both her history and her medical peculiarities—I am in debt to Professor A. E. W. Miles, F.R.C.S., honorary curator of the Odontological Museum of the Royal College of Surgeons of England, and also to Dr. Caroline Grigson, who introduced us and placed in my hands the casts (purported) of Julia Pastrana's teeth. Also to my friend Jorn Wounlund of Gothenburg, Sweden, who first told me of her whereabouts and made a long trip to Oslo, Norway, to obtain previously unpublished photographs of Julia and articles about her in the Scandinavian press. And to Mrs. Björn Lund of Oslo for the latest information about Julia; to Friederike Zeitlhofer of the Austrian Institute, New York City, for information about Friederike Gossmann, Julia's friend; and to James G. E. Smith, Ph.D., curator of North American ethnology, Museum of the American Indian, New York City, for information about "Digger Indians."

John Francis Iaderosa, assistant curator of the New York Zoological Society, evaluated for me the old tradition that Julia Pastrana was part ape and gave it a zoologist's definitive no.

Percy G. Nunn, assistant curator of the London Hospital Medical College

Museum, an authority on the Elephant Man, showed me the skeleton and memorabilia of Joseph Carey Merrick, which are preserved there, patiently answered questions, and supplied photographs. He also relayed to me the hospital's position on Michael Jackson's million-dollar offer for the skeleton. Refna Wilkin, editorial director of G. P. Putnam's Sons juvenile department, provided illustrations from my book *The Elephant Man.*

The National Neurofibromatosis Foundation, its executive director, Peter R. W. Bellermann, and its former director, Felice Yahr, were helpful with facts and trends bearing on neurofibromatosis, the Elephant Man's disorder.

Paul P. Hoffman, former head of the Archives Branch, Division of Archives and History, State of North Carolina, cleared up questions about the original Siamese twins, Chang and Eng Bunker, and furnished copies of documents and old prints.

Gaby Monet of Concepts Unlimited, Inc., New York City, generously made available still photographs from the television motion picture *Some Call Them Freaks,* which I wrote for Home Box Office and she produced and directed.

Mary Witkowski of the Historical Division, Bridgeport Public Library, Bridgeport, Connecticut, patiently verified information about the Barnum & Bailey Circus. Kenneth Holmes, one-time head of Bridgeport's Barnum Museum, where memorabilia of both Tom Thumb and P. T. Barnum are preserved, gave useful guidance.

Robert Parkinson, chief historian and librarian of the Circus World Museum, Baraboo, Wisconsin, opened up the museum's extensive files and shelves to supply old articles, books, and other material; Bill McCarthy, research historian, helped too. I also owe much to John H. Hurdle, former curator of the Ringling Museum of the Circus in Sarasota, Florida, for wise and generous advice.

A number of libraries and their staffs also helped: the Library of the Royal College of Surgeons of England and the British Library in London; the Billy Rose Theater Collection of the Library of Performing Arts, New York City; the New York Academy of Medicine; and, in Connecticut, Yale Medical Library, Yale University, New Haven, and the public libraries of Norwalk, Wilton, Westport, and Greenwich.

My friend Anatole Konstantin never let me forget there was a need for a book like this; his faith was an inspiration.

My daughter, Jean, typed the manuscript with her usual fine skill and told me a dream that she and I (and perhaps you too) will never forget. My son, John, was as always a stimulating sounding board and source of encouragement.

My wife, Evelyn, reference librarian at the Perrot Memorial Library in Old Greenwich, Connecticut, worked untiringly to locate books and information from libraries and other institutions all over the United States. She may be last on this list but she knows she is always first with me.

BORN DIFFERENT

Tom Thumb, most famous midget of all time, with his bride. Like many other very special people, they enjoyed a long and happy marriage.

Prologue

In Los Angeles one sunny afternoon two young black women were walking along Hollywood Boulevard. They were twins.

Although the pavement was crowded, wherever the two went an opening appeared as if by magic to let them pass. Several people covered their eyes. . . .

The twins came to a corner and stood there waiting to cross. Automobiles slowed down. Some screeched to a halt.

It isn't every day that you see a pair of Siamese twins strolling down Hollywood Boulevard.

Siamese twins. The crowns of the sisters' heads were joined one to the other. Totally joined. They walked bent over toward each other, their necks at an angle of nearly ninety degrees.

Yvette was the shy sister. Her face was turned slightly downward, permanently. The face of her vivacious twin, Yvonne, was turned to the side. Neither sister could look in the other's face. Yvonne was the leader because she could see ahead.

A teenager stopped and gawked. He burst into a nervous giggle. "How gross! My God, how gross!" he shrieked.

"How can they go walking in the street like that?" snarled a woman, her face white with anger. She spoke loud enough for the sisters to hear.

Directly in front of the twins three youths halted and stared, openmouthed.

"Hi, guys, how are you doing?" said Yvonne. Her brown eyes crinkled in a warm, friendly smile as she looked up at them from her bent-over, sideways position—and her voice was as warm and friendly as her smile.

Not one of the three returned her greeting. Not one stepped out of the way. They simply stood there gaping.

If Yvonne and Yvette were used to anything, it was to being stared at. They carefully backed up and moved around the youths.

Hollywood Boulevard always has its tourists. Their cameras clicked. The twins smiled.

A tall black man walked up to them. He took the hand of each twin in turn and kissed it. There were tears in his eyes.

"God bless you, sisters," the big man said to the smiling twins. He waved good-bye and was swallowed up in the crowd.

Yvonne and Yvette Jones have appeared as gospel singers before church groups. They live in Los Angeles with their mother. Most of the time they stay home. "Wherever the twins go," Mrs. Jones says, "they are greeted with love—nothing but love—once people get to know how sweet and good they are."

Mrs. Jones has received offers to exhibit her daughters at state fairs and carnivals; often that has been the only way people handicapped as they are can earn a living. She has turned all the offers down.

"My babies aren't freaks!" she cries.

It's a cruel word, "freaks."

Yet for centuries this cruel word has been used to describe—and demean—people who are formed differently from the rest of us.

They may be midgets like Tom Thumb, who, when he first appeared on the stage, stood only 25 inches high. Or giants like Robert Wadlow, who reached the astonishing height of 8 feet 11.1 inches. They may be deformed or disfigured like Joseph Merrick, the Elephant Man, or the other people whose remarkable true stories are told in these pages.

"Freaks" is a harsh word—but these people have often been called by a harsher one. The term once used by the medical profession is horrendous: "monsters." (Siamese twins were called "double monsters.") A less harmful word doctors use is "anomalies." P. T. Barnum, who made a fortune exhibiting them, referred to them as "curiosities." They are also known as "human oddities."

But still the commonest name for them is "freaks."

The word "freaks," says Anthony Burgess (he wrote *A Clockwork Orange*), "sounds like a cry of pain." Most human oddities can't stand it. They have often spoken out against it. The most striking example occurred close to a century ago, when the Barnum & Bailey Circus was beginning a historic tour of Europe. The circus sideshow, then in its heyday, had more than thirty people in it. On January 6, 1898, the performers held a protest meeting in London and called on the circus not to advertise them as freaks any longer.

The protest attracted wide attention. British newspapers called it "The Uprising of the Freaks." Although the sideshow performers didn't want to be known as "freaks," they couldn't come up with a better word. They appealed to the public for aid.

Hundreds of letters arrived with suggestions. After poring over them the sideshow committee chose one that appealed to them more than the rest. It was the word "prodigies," proposed by Canon Wilberforce of Westminster Abbey. James A. Bailey, who headed the circus (his partner, P. T. Barnum, had died), approved the choice. He ordered every one of the circus's posters to be changed, substituting "prodigies" for "freaks." An old poster in my collection portrays the members of the sideshow posing proudly above this inscription:

THE PEERLESS PRODIGIES OF PHYSICAL PHENOMENA
AND GREAT PRESENTATION OF MARVELOUS LIVING
HUMAN CURIOSITIES

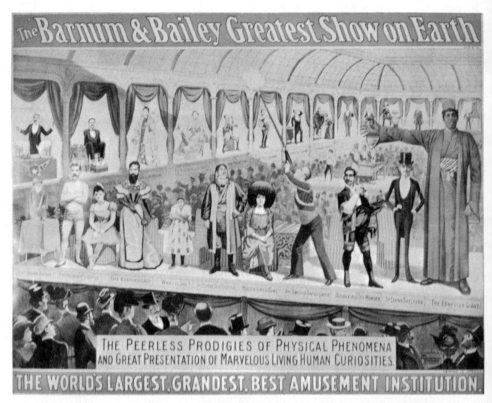

A poster printed in 1899 for the Barnum & Bailey sideshow after "The Uprising of the Freaks."

"Prodigies" they were to remain until the Greatest Show on Earth returned to the United States. Then the old familiar word crept back. The sideshow performers still loathed it and eventually it was dropped again. This time they were called "Strange People" and the sideshow itself was advertised as "The Congress of Strange People." Big circuses like Ringling Brothers gave up their sideshows years ago—tastes have changed—but at state fairs and carnivals they can still be seen; the human oddities exhibited are still billed as "Strange People."

In an earlier book I proposed another name: "Very Special People." And very special people I consider them to be. For they come into the world burdened with a special strangeness that most of them bear gallantly and with good cheer.

William Lindsay Gresham, author of *Nightmare Alley,* spent much time in carnivals and became well acquainted with many sideshow performers. He was especially impressed by those who had legs made useless by poliomyelitis, or who had lost them in accidents, and had trained themselves to perform as acrobats. What he said about them applies just as well to many other very special people.

"On their faces," wrote Gresham, "was a strangely luminous smile. I know now what it meant. They had met tragedy and fought it to a standstill; they had taken a handicap and turned it inside out, making it work for them; with courage and patience they had built themselves a life."

Another person who was greatly impressed by the very special people was Diane Arbus, a well-known photographer. Arbus took many pictures of human oddities.

"I just used to adore them," she said. "They made me feel a mixture of shame and awe. There's a quality of legend about freaks. Like a person in a fairy tale who stops you and demands that you answer a riddle. Most people go through life dreading they'll have a traumatic experience. Freaks were born with their traumas. They've already passed their test in life. They're aristocrats."

Human oddities are born with their traumas—but that's only the beginning. They have to pass not just one test in life but many.

The struggle is uphill all the way. In this book you will be witness to some of their remarkable efforts. Sometimes the simplest may be the most unforgettable—like those of the little boy born without arms who had to learn to feed, to wash, and to dress himself. Without hands! Or those of the original Siamese twins, Chang and Eng, who had to learn to do everything *together*—to walk, to run, to sleep, to eat, and, above all, to get along with each other no matter how they felt—because if they didn't their lives would be full of grief.

For a human oddity, almost as burdensome as his handicap—or handicaps—may be the effect it has on his family. The trouble starts long before he is even aware of it. Listen to a man named Stanislaw Berent, known to countless sideshow-goers as Sealo the Seal Boy because miniature hands grew out of his shoulders like a seal's flippers.

"When I was born," Berent says, "my mother looked at me and started crying."

Berent cried plenty too before he learned that crying didn't help. Like the person who has lost an arm or a leg in an accident, the human oddity has to recognize that his condition is an unchangeable fact. He has to accept it—and make the most of what he has left. The total experience is well expressed by another carnival performer, Dolly Reagan. Dolly is billed as the Half-Woman, Half-Baby; she has miniature legs and one hand permanently curled over the other and she is confined to a wheelchair.

"At the beginning," Dolly says, "it was a shock to my system. Once I made up my mind, that was *it*. I accepted my situation."

Paul Del Rio, a well-known circus performer of yesterday, put it another way. He was asked how it felt to be a midget. "You have to be," Paul replied, "what God made you."

B. J. Robinson is a carnival acrobat born without legs. His words have a sharper edge: "I try to look at everybody and say, 'I'm this way and I don't care. I dig it.' "

Because they start life with one strike against them, many of the very special people have to compete harder than the rest of us. It's not surprising that they often overcompensate. (That's one of the things that make them so special.) Herrmann Unthan, born with no arms, trained himself to be a fine violinist, to play the cornet, to swim and dive, to shoot expertly, to write (you will see a beautifully written letter of his later)—all with his legs and feet. He had adapted so superbly to his situation that he could say, "If a miracle happened and I suddenly found I had sprouted a pair of arms I wouldn't know what to do with them." After you read his story you'll believe him.

Julia Pastrana was known as the Ugliest Woman in the World.

Sometimes people fainted when she smiled at them. Yet she succeeded in making herself celebrated on two continents for her lovely singing and dancing. The young giant Robert Wadlow took lessons in public speaking to conquer his shyness and became a successful promoter, earning a good income for himself and his family. (Many of the very special people are the sole support of large families.) By endlessly honing his skills in the performing arts, Tom Thumb transformed himself from a stammering country boy into the most famous midget who ever lived.

Robert Wadlow, the tallest man who ever lived, made a good living for himself and his family by promoting shoes.

Other examples abound. For one very notable one, consider Harry Bulson, born with useless legs. Brought up near Paterson, New Jersey, as a child Harry played by himself, afraid to face other children. He taught himself to walk on his hands and then to travel through the trees, swinging from branch to branch like Tarzan. One of his boyhood pastimes (not an especially praiseworthy one) was catching birds. He set traps for them in the trees, holding on to a branch with his teeth.

Bulson's sufferings made him seem queer and he was placed in a mental institution. His hands were so powerful he was able to twist the bars in his window and escape. He was found and brought back. He escaped a second time and was brought back. He escaped a third time. A lonely old man took the unhappy boy in and gave him a home. A visit to a carnival launched him on a career.

In the carnival, living with other human prodigies like himself, Bulson could at last feel he was among people who didn't look down upon him. He could take pride in his self-taught skills as an acrobat and a contortionist. He hardened himself against the insensitive remarks, the curious stares of spectators. As the Spider Boy, he became one of Coney Island's greatest sideshow attractions in the 1930s. He made the *Ripley's Believe It or Not* series twice. One time it was because he walked a mile on his hands in forty-two minutes thirty seconds. Another time, with his powerful teeth, he lifted a car weighing 3,850 pounds. When Lon Chaney played the role of Quasimodo in *The Hunchback of Notre Dame* Bulson took Chaney's place whenever dangerous stunts had to be performed.

B. J. Robinson, mentioned earlier (he is now in his thirties and can be seen performing at state fairs), was born without legs. Like the Spider Boy, he walks on his hands. His arms, his shoulders, and his neck are powerfully muscled from years as an acrobat. To join the sideshow, he hitchhiked all the way to Gainesville, Florida, from San Francisco—traveling on a skateboard when he couldn't get a lift.

As a child, B. J. was fitted with artificial legs. At sixteen he gave them up. "I get around better without them, and here in the side-show nobody thinks about it."

As a boy, Carl Sandburg, a famous writer and folksinger, paid his dime (this was a long time ago) and walked into a sideshow. Looking at the human oddities there, young Carl felt unhappy. "They seemed to me to be mistakes that God had made; that God was absentminded when he shaped them. I hung around the midget and his wife, watched them sign their names to photographs they sold at ten cents—and they were that pleasant and witty that I saw I had guessed wrong about them and they were having . . . fun out of life. . . ."

Many human oddities not only have fun—they develop an outstanding sense of humor. (If they didn't learn to grin and bear it they might go under.) Tom Thumb, Barnum's premier midget, was celebrated for his lively wit; a few of the people who enjoyed bantering with him were Queen Victoria, the duke of Wellington, the czar of Russia, and Abraham Lincoln. Robert Wadlow, who suffered from serious physical problems because of his rapid, endless growth, was a cheerful, good hearted fellow with a multitude of friends; he kept audiences of thousands in stitches with anecdotes that made fun of his height. Chang and Eng, the Siamese twins, were renowned for their quick repartee; the examples in these pages still make people laugh. Lady Olga, a Ringling Brothers sideshow star, was famous not just for her whiskers but for her wit. She was once asked whether she would take part in New York City's Easter Parade. "I most certainly will not parade on Fifth Avenue," Olga replied, stroking her graying beard. "Somebody's likely to mistake me for a Supreme Court judge."

In an interview B. J. Robinson said, "I just want to be a regular person, run a regular life." He said he might marry someday. And the fact is that many human prodigies do marry. Sometimes, like Tom Thumb, they choose people of their own kind. But more frequently they marry "normals."

The marriages of human oddities are usually more lasting than those of "normals." (Very likely the relationship means more to them because they have spent so many years in loneliness.) Chang and Eng married sisters, lived happily with them all their lives, and had a surprising number of children. Herrmann Unthan had an idyllic marriage. So did, and do, others even more severely handicapped. Kobelkoff, known as the Human Trunk because he had neither arms nor legs, had a good family life: he fathered eleven children. Prince Randian, the Caterpillar Man, who had the same handicap (in spite of it he could shave himself and roll cigarettes), had five children and many grandchildren.

I hope that, if you didn't before, you have begun to see that human oddities are just as human as the rest of us. They think like us and they feel like us. Except for the difference in their bodies they are as "normal" as anybody else. They want to be treated just like anybody else. That point was forcefully brought home to me by my daughter, Jean, some years ago when she was doing research for me.

Jean had been looking at countless photographs of human oddities and reading about them. Their lot in life made such a strong impression on her that one night she dreamed about it. Because her dream was so unusual—and so full of meaning—I feel I should tell you about it. This is how she recalled it:

"In my dream I was all alone. I was walking down a strange street in a strange town.

"Out of nowhere a crowd of men, women, and children appeared. They swirled around me. . . .

"Suddenly I noticed the children were pointing their fingers at me. The men began to laugh. The women turned away or covered their eyes. Horror twisted their faces.

"I examined myself all over. I didn't have far to look.

"My arms had disappeared.

"In their place, growing directly out of my shoulders, were two very small, slender hands.

"But otherwise I was the same person I had always been. I

certainly felt the same.

" 'Stop looking at me like that!' I cried to the people surrounding me. 'What if I am physically different from you? I'm still a human being like you. Treat me like one. I have the same feelings—exactly the same feelings as you.

" 'I am you!' "

Tom Thumb at the start of his career, with his proud father, Sherwood Stratton.

The Most Famous Dwarf
Who Ever Lived

It was Charlie's first birthday. His mother should have been happy, but how could she be? Giving her beautiful blond-haired little boy a tight hug, Cynthia laid him tenderly on the scale.

The child laughed his pleasure. To him it was a game she played with him almost every day and he loved the special closeness of her embrace before she set him on the scale.

For Cynthia it was no game. She prayed. Then she began to pile the weights on the other side.

The last weight clunked in place. The scale came into balance.

Fifteen pounds. Poor little Charlie hadn't gained an ounce in months. In seven months, in fact.

But perhaps he'd grown! Her eyes bright with hope, she set him on his feet. She cautioned him to stand up straight.

If he was short in size he wasn't short in understanding. Charlie stood as erect as he was able while Cynthia ran the tape measure from his heel to the shining crown of his head.

Not a fraction of an inch taller either.

Why had her little boy stopped growing? Other children the same age weighed twice as much and they kept shooting upward. Her two daughters were completely normal, good-sized girls.

At birth Charlie had been a big, lovely baby, weighing over nine pounds. Everything about him was just as it was supposed to be. He had put on weight rapidly. He had added inch after inch. Then, abruptly, in his fifth month, he'd stopped gaining. And he'd also stopped growing.

Before she knew it, Charlie had reached his second birthday and his weight, his height hadn't increased a bit. At three it was the same. And again at four. A handsome, healthy, perfectly proportioned boy, he stood just twenty-five inches tall—and he still weighed an unbelievable fifteen pounds. Her husband, Sherwood, flushed as he carried the miniature child down the church aisle on Sunday. The boy could toddle along well enough—but what man wanted to be seen walking with a son so tiny he didn't even reach his father's knee?

By now Cynthia had grudgingly found the courage to face the terrible truth: Her son was a dwarf.

For Charlie, things any normal-sized boy his age could do for himself were—and evidently forever would be—completely impossible.

If a door had to be opened, he couldn't open it; the handle was simply beyond his reach. The lowest chair in the house was too high for him—although by wriggling and struggling gallantly he could finally pull himself up on it. Even then his mother had to place a cushion under him; otherwise his head would be below the tabletop and he couldn't feed himself.

Worst of all was when he wanted to play with other children his age. "Baby, baby!" they cried. "Go home, baby!" When he refused to leave, he was punched and kicked until he had to give up.

Of other problems there were plenty. On raw, blustery days, for example, Charlie's mother could not let him go out of doors by himself: she was afraid a sudden strong gust of wind might fling him in the path of an oncoming horse and carriage. An ordinary-sized dog was as big as a lion to him and its bark could terrify him.

Even so, his disposition was as bright and sunny as his hair.

The dwarf's name was Charles Sherwood Stratton and he had

been born January 4, 1838, in Bridgeport, a drowsy little Connecticut town. His mother, Cynthia, was of above-average height. His father, Sherwood, a carpenter, stood six feet tall. Sherwood turned out regularly to drill with the militia, as his father and his grandfather had done before him back to Revolutionary days. But his eyes misted over when they fell on his puny son, who would never be able to shoulder a musket and take his place manfully in the Connecticut line.

To Cynthia and Sherwood Stratton it had come as a shock that their son was so different from other boys. Like Americans of their time, in their heart of hearts they felt the child's misfortune must be due to some sin on their part. It was a punishment they must in some way have deserved. Because the boy needed them more than their daughters did, they loved him the more, but they never stopped brooding about him.

What would become of little Charlie when he "grew up"? He certainly couldn't follow in his father's man-sized trade. What kind of life could he make for himself in a little, quiet place like Bridgeport, a town of farmers and whaling men? Who would take care of him when his parents were gone?

Often, at night, in bed, Cynthia suddenly burst into tears, worrying about her unlucky son's future, and Sherwood, trying to comfort her, would find himself crying with her.

One wintry day in 1842, when Charlie was almost five, an ambitious young showman stopped off in Bridgeport. His name was Phineas T. Barnum. Later in his life P. T. Barnum would become famous as part-owner of a celebrated circus, which he would call "The Greatest Show on Earth," and his name would become a household word. In 1842, however, he was almost unknown.

Barnum had just bought a showplace, the American Museum, in New York City. In that age public museums like the ones we have today simply did not exist. Barnum's museum was a combination zoo, natural history museum, theater, and hodgepodge of curiosities from all over the world. In it he had live animals and he had stuffed ones. He had portraits of great Americans, a working model of Niagara Falls, the arm of a dead pirate, and a knitting machine operated by a patient dog. He also had human oddities—giants, living skeletons, and others so unlike the common run of mankind that they were called by the unkind name of freaks.

When P. T. Barnum stopped in Bridgeport he was searching for new features that might help attract the public to his American Museum. The showman soon heard there was a boy in town so tiny he amazed everyone who saw him. He immediately asked to meet the child.

When Charlie Stratton was brought in, Barnum's eyes opened wide. He had seen plenty of dwarfs before, but never one so small and attractive as this one.

Too bashful to speak to a stranger, Charlie hung back at first. The showman, however, had children of his own, and he knew how to win a little boy's confidence. He quickly made friends with Charlie, and in no time at all the child was chattering away as if he'd known the tall stranger all his life.

Barnum saw the little fellow was remarkably bright and winning and decided to take a chance on him. He asked Mrs. Stratton if she would care to bring her son to New York City for a four-week trial at his museum and he offered to pay her three dollars a week and all of her and Charlie's expenses.

A dollar in 1842 was worth many times what a dollar is today. Three dollars was more than Charlie's hard-working father earned in some weeks. The Strattons could scarcely believe their good fortune.

P. T. Barnum was a genius of advertising long before advertising became a profession. He realized that for a show to be successful it needed to be presented or "packaged" with imagination. Americans were a simple, homespun people who thought anything from a foreign country had to be better than anything at home— otherwise why would anyone have taken the trouble to bring it across the sea? It would never do to tell the public Charlie was an

The celebrated showman P. T. Barnum poses with his "protégé," Tom Thumb.

American boy from nearby Connecticut. Instead Barnum decided he would announce his dwarf was English, and he had just stepped off the boat from Europe.

Charlie's real name, Barnum also decided, was just too ordinary. He needed a new name, one so unusual it would make people want to see him.

From old nursery rhymes almost everybody had learned about a gallant little knight of King Arthur's court named Sir Thomas Thumb. Sir Thomas was no bigger than a thumb—so tiny he rode to battle not on a horse, like any self-respecting knight, but on a mouse. No match for fire-breathing dragons, he did battle with spiders instead, fighting them with a needle in place of the regulation sword.

Tom Thumb, it seemed to Barnum, would be an appealing comic name for Charlie. To make it more comic still, the showman tacked the title of general in front of it. The dwarf, when he walked out on P. T.'s stage, would no longer be Charles Sherwood Stratton but General Tom Thumb, Jr.

How old should Barnum say the general was? From Charlie's speech and movements anyone could tell he was no more than a child. Actually he wasn't even five. But to reveal his true age might make people wonder whether he was a real dwarf or simply a child whose growth was slow. With a stroke of the pen Barnum more than doubled the boy's age, declaring he was eleven.

One bothersome question still remained: How would General Tom Thumb, Jr., entertain the public? The child could sing prettily enough but that was about all. Barnum had traveled with road shows and was an experienced entertainer himself. He personally gave the boy lessons in singing and dancing. He taught him to act and do imitations of famous people. Flattered by all the attention his big new friend was showing him, Charlie practiced until he was ready to drop. As for Barnum, he was delighted to discover his protégé was a quick learner, with unusual talent and a natural gift for comedy. Like a bud that had been waiting for the sun, the child's

Barnum training Tom Thumb. The illustration is from the showman's autobiography.

personality opened up and bloomed under the warmth of Barnum's encouragement.

It was Charlie's premiere. Barnum and Cynthia watched anxiously as the tiny child toddled out on the stage of the American Museum dressed in the colorful, stately uniform of a general of the Revolutionary War. Almost immediately the audience exploded in laughter and exclamations of delight. Who could resist the cocky little fellow, with his comic ways, his pert, bright face, his eagerness to please? Mothers and fathers fell in love with him at first sight because he was no bigger than a baby. Children identified with him because he was even smaller than they were, and they howled at his clowning and his hilarious antics.

To make sure his new performer wouldn't get stage fright, P. T. appeared in the show with him. But almost from the start he could see Charlie was born for the theater. He sang and strutted, he mimicked and mimed with the natural ease of someone who had been before the footlights all his life.

Barnum always made a point of showing the audience how tiny the general was. Early in the act he would ask for a little boy to come up on the stage and sit next to the dwarf on his special small sofa.

"Mr. Barnum," piped up Tom Thumb, "I'd rather have a little miss."

"A little miss? I agree." Barnum quickly located a girl who was willing to come up on the stage.

"You needn't be afraid, miss," squeaked Tom Thumb's tiny voice as she walked forward.

Barnum invited the girl to sit down on the sofa. All smiles, Tom Thumb scrambled up and took his place by her side. The audience gasped. How incredibly minute he looked next to her!

Barnum cleared his throat. "Well, General, how do you progress with your courtship?"

"First rate, sir." The midget winked mischievously.

"Is the little miss in any way bashful?"

"A little, sir."

"Well, you must encourage her as well as you can."

"I'll try, sir." And reaching up his round little cherub's face, the general planted a kiss on the girl's cheek. She hugged him warmly and sat him on her lap like a doll. Roars of laughter shook the theater.

Day after day Tom Thumb's performances packed the American Museum as it had seldom been packed before. In just his first six weeks thirty thousand people lined up to pay their quarters and watch him perform. Barnum, overjoyed, raised the boy's pay and gave him a year's contract. From that day, if Cynthia and Sherwood Stratton ever sighed about their son, they were sighs not of worry but contentment. Never again would they lie awake in the gloom brooding about their little son's future.

Other cities heard about the remarkable midget and wanted to see him. Barnum sent his little general on a tour up and down the

East Coast. With him traveled his mother, his father (who gave up carpentering to be his son's ticket taker), a tutor, and a dancing master hired to teach the little star new routines. Everywhere his performances were a sellout. At the end of each show a crowd of women and girls remained, eager to hug and kiss their tiny darling. On a tour of the South, according to Barnum, the general was kissed by sixty thousand. For the boy who only a few months before had felt so lonely and friendless, a completely new life had opened up. Now, wherever he went, he was pursued by packs of admirers.

For a year P. T. Barnum exhibited his miniature man in New York City and around the country. Tom Thumb's success was so enormous the showman was getting rich. With such a little gold mine on his hands he began to wonder about new places to exhibit him. If Americans loved the gifted midget so much, why, Barnum asked himself, shouldn't the people in foreign countries like England and France find him just as appealing? Surely there must be a fortune waiting to be made on the other side of the Atlantic.

No sooner did Barnum have an idea than he began to carry it out. In January 1844, he embarked for England with his protégé. The American Museum's brass band escorted the party (which included the general's parents) to the dock. Thousands lined the streets of lower Manhattan to wave good-bye to their fair-haired little hero.

It took nineteen days by swift sailing ship to reach Liverpool, on the west coast of England. When the ship docked the pier was crowded.

The newspapers must have announced they were coming, exulted Barnum. Well, no one was going to see General Tom Thumb unless they paid for the privilege. He told Charlie's mother to wrap the boy up in a blanket and carry him ashore in her arms like a baby so no one would recognize him.

The little general peered out over the top of his blanket. His heart pounded as he got his first sight of this strange foreign land. Here, Mr. Barnum had promised, he would have his greatest triumph.

That evening a showman called at their hotel. He said he owned a small waxworks and he wanted Tom Thumb and his manager to appear there. Dwarfs were very commonplace in sideshows, he explained, and he couldn't charge more than a few pennies admission. But for the great Tom Thumb he was willing to pay the grand sum of ten dollars a week. Barnum was shocked. He was already paying Tom Thumb five times that amount!

England, it seemed, was not waiting eagerly to shower its treasure on P. T. Barnum and his little general. It hardly knew they existed. That night the usually cheerful, talkative showman sat glum and silent at dinner and turned in early. In bed he brooded that he had made a terrible mistake; his English venture was doomed to failure. He had brought letters of introduction to influential people but hadn't had a chance to deliver them. "Beyond my own little circle," he wrote later, "I had not seen a friendly face. . . . I was 'blue,' homesick, almost in despair."

In the next few days the Americans' prospects began to look brighter. Barnum delivered his letters and made many new friends. They persuaded him to hire a hall in Liverpool and present the little general to the public. The showman had intended to go directly to London and exhibit the general at Buckingham Palace, before the young queen herself. But the royal family was in mourning. No entertainer could be presented to Queen Victoria. Barnum would have to wait.

Tom Thumb's show in Liverpool attracted a London theater manager, who engaged him to appear in the capital. But the London engagement was a disappointment. The little general was only a minor feature, performing during an intermission in an opera. Barnum was dissatisfied. The showman wanted "to bring him before the public, on my own account and in my own time and way."

First, however, he would have to make the general better known. With classic Yankee shrewdness, he began to launch his campaign.

In Mayfair, the most fashionable section of London, Barnum

rented a handsome mansion and hired servants to staff it. Then he made a list of the most important people of the city—editors, lords and ladies, and other persons of influence or wealth—and sent them invitations to come and meet Tom Thumb, the Smallest Man in the World, who had newly arrived from the United States.

Just as Americans had been curious about the remarkable novelty from Britain, the British upper classes were curious about the general when they were told he came from the States. They were always searching for something new and different to see and do. Soon the streets near the Barnum residence were lined with elegant carriages, many decorated with the crests of the noblest families in the land. The little carpenter's son from Connecticut found himself taking tea with baronets and counts, with dukes and earls, with editors, with bankers and their wives. He hobnobbed with them and he joked with them almost as easily as if they were back-home folks he'd known all his life.

As for the guests, never before had they met anyone quite like the general. They were amazed at his unbelievably small size, and enchanted by his quaint, familiar, Yankee ways and his funny American speech. Soon their friends and their friends' friends were clamoring to be invited to meet him too.

Before long it was Barnum's turn to receive an invitation. This one came from Baroness Rothschild, wife of the richest banker in the world. A few evenings afterward she sent her carriage to bring General Tom Thumb to perform at a gathering in her mansion. When the evening's entertainment was at an end, a well-filled purse was placed in the showman's hand.

"The golden shower had begun to fall," Barnum wrote later. Soon after, a visit to the mansion of another prominent banker "came to the same golden conclusion."

Barnum decided the time was now ripe to try Tom Thumb's luck in the theater again. He engaged a room at the Egyptian Hall, a famous London showplace, and Tom Thumb began to appear there. Meanwhile the showman had been pulling strings to win an

GENERAL TOM THUMB, *1844*

The celebrated American Dwarf, exhibiting every day and evening, at the Egyptian Hall, Piccadilly.

CHARLES S. STRATTON, known as General Tom Thumb, was born January 11, 1832, consequently he is now twelve years of age: he is twenty-five inches high, and weighs only fifteen pounds. The General had the honour of appearing before Her Majesty, Prince Albert, the Duchess of Kent, and several of the Nobility, at Buckingham Palace, attended by his guardian, Mr. P. T. Barnum, of New York, on Saturday, 23d of March. His various performances afforded much entertainment, and elicited the approbation of Her Majesty and the Royal Household.

The General is of the most symmetrical proportions, active, lively, intelligent, and sociable. He is robust and hearty, never having been ill in his life. His parents and a preceptor have accompanied him across the Atlantic. The extreme diminutiveness—the graceful bearing and fascinating manners of this beautiful rosy-cheeked MAN in miniature—cannot be justly conceived without seeing him. The General has been visited in America and the Canadas by nearly half a million of ladies and gentlemen of the first respectability, who unanimously pronounce him the greatest curiosity in the world.

The General shed his first set of teeth several years since; and his enormous strength, his firm and manly gait, establish his age beyond all dispute. The General amuses his Visitors with a relation of his History, Songs, Dances, Imitation of Napoleon Buonaparte, Grecian Statues, &c.

Left: Tom Thumb as Napoleon Bonaparte, during his London appearance. The text purposely misstates the midget's age. *Right:* An advertisement announcing Tom Thumb's last week at Barnum's American Museum. The midget had many such "last weeks" before he finally sailed for England in January 1844.

audience for his protégé before the queen. He visited the American ambassador in London, Edward Everett, and the ambassador and his family fell in love with the little man. Ambassador Everett introduced Tom and Barnum to a member of the queen's personal staff.

The Englishman was delighted with the general and he was sure the queen would be too. He promised to bring the little American to Her Majesty's attention without delay.

One morning, a tall officer in a scarlet coat and bright steel helmet rapped on Barnum's door, handed the butler an envelope, saluted, and left. Barnum took it. The little general heard him whoop with joy. Then Barnum showed him the envelope. He pointed to a crown of gold on the outside and the letters *V R* beneath.

V R. That stood for Victoria Regina—Victoria the Queen. Barnum opened the letter with great care and read the queen's invitation for General Tom Thumb and his "guardian" to appear before Her Majesty at Buckingham Palace.

How many days are so important that we remember them all the rest of our lives? For Tom Thumb the evening of March 23, 1844, was one he would never forget. He would never forget riding with Mr. Barnum through the gates of Buckingham Palace while the guardsmen stood at attention. He would never forget how tight the showman held him as he carried him down a long magnificent corridor and up a broad staircase of marble.

Barnum stopped before a tall doorway and set the little general on his feet. The doors were thrown open and the midget stepped gingerly inside.

The chamber was vast; to the pygmy general it seemed to stretch for miles and miles. Hundreds of paintings of every size and shape crowded the walls from floor to ceiling. At the far end he saw a cluster of lords and ladies, all richly dressed. In their midst he recognized from their pictures the young queen, dressed in black, and her handsome husband, Prince Albert. Bits of lively conversation drifted to the boy. Suddenly it died out as the group noticed the tiny figure that had just entered the great chamber.

The little general's heart was beating so fiercely he felt a pounding in his ears.

Never before, he knew, had so much depended on the impression he would make.

He hesitated. He glanced back to reassure himself that Mr. Barnum was close behind him. Then, raising his chin and straightening his back, he marched forward.

When he stood in front of the group he paused and made a deep bow.

"Good evening, ladies and gentlemen!" he piped in his bright little voice, his button eyes sparkling with excitement.

The lords, in their fashionable dinner jackets and bemedaled scarlet uniforms, and the ladies in their elegant gowns of silk and satin, instantly burst into giggles like a bunch of schoolchildren. Queen Victoria laughed until the tears shone in her eyes, and so did her tall husband, Prince Albert.

No one loved children more than the queen, who had three small ones of her own. Her heart went out to the little tyke before her. Rising, she took him by the hand and, walking with him, asked him a hundred questions about himself. His answers made her and the whole party laugh merrily.

The chamber was the royal picture gallery, and Queen Victoria pointed out pictures of her ancestors to the general and told him about them. The general had been in great houses before, but even he was impressed. He informed her that her paintings were "first rate."

He asked if he could see her son, the three-year-old Prince of Wales. The prince was in bed, but she promised the general could see him another time. Her lord-in-waiting was sent to bring some chocolates, and she fed these to the dwarf with her own hand. She questioned Barnum about the general's education and warned the showman not to strain the boy beyond his mental powers. (She believed that midgets, because they were small, had limited mental capacity, a common error of the time.)

The queen and her friends formed a circle around the general and he began to perform. He danced a hornpipe, sang, danced, did an imitation of Napoleon, and told some of his most popular jokes. His noble audience kept clapping and cheering him on. They found him as much a delight as the most homespun Americans had.

An hour had passed like a minute and the visit was at an end. Custom required that the visitors bow to the queen and, while facing her, walk backward toward the door. Barnum bowed first, followed by the general. The showman, with his giant strides, quickly covered much of the gallery's length. The general, backing away on his short legs, sensed his tall friend was no longer close by. Afraid he might be left behind, he suddenly swung around and ran a few steps after Barnum. Then, remembering where he was, he faced about, bowed again to the smiling queen, and continued to back away. In an instant he turned around again, ran several steps, then turned about and bowed.

Barnum himself could not have staged a funnier scene—funnier, that is, to all but one. The queen's poodle had never seen anyone behave so disrespectfully in the royal presence. Yapping furiously, the dog launched itself at the boy.

The sudden attack caught the general off guard. Instinctively he raised the little cane he carried and shook it threateningly at the dog to make it keep its distance. Then he quickly turned about and raced off after Barnum, running into his outstretched arms. The loud laughter of the queen and her guests filled the great gallery.

Next morning, over its toast and tea, all London read about Tom Thumb's audience at Buckingham Palace and the pleasure it had given the queen. The little general's name was on everybody's tongue. A long line quickly formed outside the Egyptian Hall to buy tickets for his show. Business became so brisk Barnum had to rent the largest hall in the building. Every performance was packed.

Almost unknown before, Tom Thumb was now a national celebrity. Newspapers printed his picture and called him "the pet of the palace." He was invited to come back and entertain the royal

E. SEARS.

Pandemonium in the palace. Tom Thumb puts up a stout defense against an attack from the queen's poodle.

family again and again. The queen dowager, the czar of Russia (who was visiting London), the great peers of the kingdom asked him to perform for them. Each of them paid Barnum handsomely. They also gave the midget presents of valuable jewels, which were proudly displayed in the hall where the general was performing. Between his appearances on the stage and at private parties, he was possibly the busiest six-year-old in history.

After London, Barnum took his star on a tour of the major cities of England, Scotland, and Ireland. Tom Thumb's act was constantly changed to appeal to local audiences. In Scotland he spoke with a burr, wore a kilt, and danced the Highland fling. In Ireland he put on a brogue and danced an Irish jig. Everywhere women and girls lined up at the end of his show to hug and kiss him.

The public knew very little about dwarfs. They usually were greatly surprised when they learned that Tom Thumb's parents and his sisters were persons of normal height. Once, for example, an elderly lady was introduced to Tom Thumb's six-foot father. "Is that tiny, tiny creature really your son?" she asked in astonishment.

"Well," replied Sherwood Stratton, "I have to support him."

"I rather think," said the lady, "that he supports you."

She had, of course, hit the nail squarely on the head. Many dwarfs, giants, bearded ladies and other human oddities in show business have been the chief support of their entire families, and Tom Thumb was no exception. His father was rapidly becoming a wealthy man with the money his son was earning.

Near the end of their British tour Barnum had a coach made for his protégé by the queen's own carriage maker. Built to the general's proportions, it was just thirty-four inches high and it was painted a patriotic red, white, and blue; on its door was Barnum's motto: "GO AHEAD!" To pull it, the showman bought four little Shetland ponies and hired two boys to serve as coachman and foot-

The miniature man used to ride about in his tiny coach to advertise his performances.

man. Whenever Tom Thumb was to appear in a town, he first rode about in his tiny coach, a living advertisement for his performances.

After his great success in Britain, Tom Thumb was taken to France. His reputation had traveled before him. In Paris, besides his public performances, he gave private ones for King Louis Philippe and his family as well as for the rich and powerful. He had been studying French very hard, and now a play was written for him in which he played the role of a clever dwarf who outwitted a cruel giant. The instant the doll-like boy stepped out on the stage and spoke his first word of French the hearts of the audience were his. As in Britain, he became a popular favorite. Plaster statuettes of the general were sold in the stores and children munched figures of chocolate in his shape. Snuffboxes with pictures of Tom Thumb on the cover could be seen in many hands.

After a tour of France Tom Thumb and his party were off to Spain. The queen, who was only a girl herself, hugged him, planted a warm kiss on his lips, and carried him off to see a bullfight with her. In Belgium, too, he was coddled by the rulers and applauded by the common people. On a return trip to Britain he made a greater hit than before.

After three years in Europe, Barnum decided it was time to bring the general home. He was not only a rich boy of nine now, he was a very worldly-wise one.

"I have traveled fifty thousand miles," he told an admirer, "been before more crowned heads than any other Yankee living, except my friend Mr. Barnum, and have kissed nearly two millions of ladies, including the queens of England, France, Belgium, and Spain."

It was a remark he was to make again and again. Never would he suggest, however, that he enjoyed all the hugging and kissing. It was just something he had to submit to in the theater or at a private party because it pleased his patrons. If he happened to be on the street and some motherly soul recognized him and tried to take him

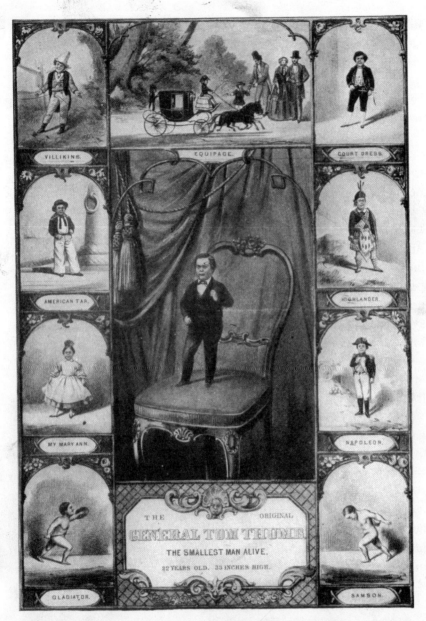

The little general in some of the roles he made famous, portrayed in a Currier and Ives print. Americans bought thousands of prints like this one.

in her arms, he would tear himself free and run away as fast as his short legs would carry him. Enough was enough.

Not many people know it, but midgets usually grow with the years. Certainly this was true of Tom Thumb. By the time he reached age twenty-four he stood thirty-five inches high and weighed fifty-two pounds. To show the world he was no longer a child but a man, he grew a mustache.

Tom Thumb performed under his own management now. But he and P. T. Barnum remained the best of friends and he sometimes made appearances at the American Museum. He had been received by President and Mrs. James Polk at the White House and was one of the best-known and most successful theatrical personalities in America. He owned real estate, pedigreed horses, even a yacht. His father had passed away; but his permanent home was still in Bridgeport, where he lived with his mother in a big attractive house built with his money, in rooms especially equipped for a person his size. (You can see some of his midget furnishings if you visit the Barnum Museum in Bridgeport.)

In 1862 Barnum was featuring two midgets at his American Museum. One was a handsome little man called Commodore Nutt, the other an exquisite little woman named Lavinia Warren.

Born in 1841 in Middleboro, Massachusetts, Lavinia in her early twenties weighed just twenty-nine pounds and stood a scant thirty-two inches high. Her parents were tall, like Tom Thumb's, and she had four brothers and two sisters of normal height, but another sister, Minnie, was shorter than she was. Lavinia (or Vinnie as she was called) had once taught school, where she was smaller than even the smallest of her pupils. She had also appeared with a troupe of entertainers on a Mississippi showboat, but the Civil War had brought that part of her career to an end.

When Tom Thumb met Lavinia Warren he thought she was the loveliest little woman he had ever seen. Almost at once he knew he had to have her for his wife. Although he had kissed or been kissed by more women than anyone else on earth, he suddenly became very shy when he had to court a lady his own size. He appealed to P. T. Barnum for help.

"Mr. Barnum," he said excitedly, "you've always been a friend of mine and I want you to say a good word for me to her."

Barnum thought this was too sudden a passion. "You must do your own courting," he said. He pointed out that Commodore Nutt would be his rival. "And more than that, Miss Warren is nobody's fool and you will have to proceed very cautiously in winning her affections."

Undismayed, the general began a campaign to win Lavinia's affection. He called on her regularly at the American Museum. Each time he came he brought a big package of candy or flowers, or some other gift. It didn't take Lavinia long to figure out what was on his mind.

Commodore Nutt was not blind to Tom Thumb's intentions either. After having been an admirer of the older, more famous midget, he now could barely conceal his resentment. One day when the two little men were together at the museum an argument flared up between them. Before the general realized what was happening, he felt a sharp blow on his chin and found himself lying on the floor in a daze. The commodore was lighter, faster on his feet, and skilled in the art of boxing. This, the general decided, was one fight he did not care to continue.

Tom Thumb had lost the battle but not the war. Before long Lavinia gave him her hand. The little commodore was a good loser. He even agreed to serve as best man at Tom Thumb's wedding. Privately he told Barnum, "My fruit is plucked." (He appears to have never married.)

The announcement of the engagement of the two dwarfs aroused wide interest. Barnum saw an opportunity to cash in on it and he engaged Tom Thumb to appear with his bride-to-be at the American Museum. Day after day the showplace bulged with people who came to gawk at the bridal couple.

As the wedding day drew closer, Barnum felt he must make an

effort to hold on to his two little stars. He offered the general and Lavinia fifteen thousand dollars if they would postpone the wedding for a month and continue the exhibition at the museum.

The general's eyes flashed fire. "Not for fifty thousand dollars!" he cried.

His lovely fiancée nodded vigorous agreement. "Good for you, Charlie! Only you should have said not for a *hundred thousand!*"

The wedding of the dwarfs was the social event of the year. It took place at Grace Church in New York City on February 10, 1863—and who should be in charge but P. T. Barnum. The demand for invitations was enormous. Barnum issued two thousand of them. The guests included senators, generals, and social leaders like the Vanderbilts, the Astors, and the Roosevelts. A special platform was erected before the altar so everyone in the church could watch Tom and Lavinia take their vows. Lavinia's sister Minnie and Commodore Nutt stood solemnly beside them. (For years Barnum

Wedding of the midgets. Flanking the happy bride and groom are Tom's former rival, Commodore Nutt, and the sister of the bride, Minnie Warren.

was to feature at his museum life-sized wax figures of the wedding party.)

Afterward the streets were black with carriages hurrying to the reception, at a hotel nearby. Tom Thumb and his radiant bride were lifted onto a grand piano so they could shake hands with their guests as they filed by. They had an enormous wedding cake, from which Lavinia saved a piece that she treasured all her life. Among the wedding gifts were presents from some of the nation's most prominent people, including an elegant set of Chinese fire screens from Mrs. Abraham Lincoln, wife of the president. The Civil War was blazing across the country, but to New York's newspapers the wedding of the dwarfs was the big news that day.

For their honeymoon the Thumbs journeyed to Philadelphia, Baltimore, and Washington, D.C. In the capital the president gave a reception in their honor at the White House. To it he invited the members of his cabinet and leading people in the government, with their families, so they might forget for a few hours the terrible tragedy of the war.

The eyes of everyone were on the happy bride and groom. Lavinia looked lovely in her long-trained wedding gown of white satin and lace, Tom Thumb handsomer than ever in his full-dress suit. Tad Lincoln, the president's young son, personally carried refreshments to the little guests of honor.

President Lincoln seated Mr. and Mrs. Thumb between himself and Mrs. Lincoln. No one admired Lavinia's beauty more than he did—she reminded him of Mrs. Lincoln in earlier, more joyful days. His craggy face, often so sad, lit up with a sunny smile as he beheld the happiness of the dwarfs. In a jolly mood, he poked fun at Tom Thumb.

"You are now the great center of attention, General," Lincoln told him. "You've thrown me completely in the shade. As a military man, what's your opinion of the war?"

Even in the most distinguished company Tom Thumb was seldom at a loss for a smart reply. "Mr. President," he replied, "my friend Mr. Barnum would settle the whole affair in a month."

"General," asked the secretary of war, laughing, "have you ever been called upon to do active duty in the field?"

He intended it to be a humorous question. But it couldn't have been very funny to Tom Thumb, since it could only remind him how different he was from other men. Fortunately he didn't have to answer; the president replied for him. "General Thumb's duty is now needed in the matrimonial field. He will serve in the home guard."

The six-foot-four president stood up next to Tom Thumb and turned to his son. "Tad," he said, "God likes to do things in funny ways." He pointed a gnarled finger at himself and then at the general. "Here you have the long and the short of it."

An extensive tour took the Thumbs to Europe with Minnie and

With Minnie Warren and Commodore Nutt, the Thumbs formed a touring company that traveled around the globe. (Note the changes in height since the wedding.)

Commodore Nutt. Later, in 1869, the two couples made a tour of the entire world, visiting such faraway places as Australia and Japan, and were received by kings, princes, and the pope. When they returned home, happy but exhausted, they reported they had traveled 56,000 miles and given 1,471 performances.

The Thumbs seemed very contented in their marriage. One thing, and one thing only, was missing to make their happiness complete. It was often reported they were the parents of a little girl, and when they traveled under Barnum's management they sometimes appeared with a baby. The child looked so big that people wondered how the midgets could hold it. The baby wasn't their own, however, but one hired by Barnum to give the show greater human interest. Although the Thumbs would have dearly loved to have a child of their own, they never did.

For Tom Thumb, just seeing children was a treat. He seldom passed children at play without stopping. "Vinnie," he once said to his wife, "I love to watch them. You know, I never had any childhood, any boy-life." It was no exaggeration. Barnum had taken the midget when he was only four years old—and from that time on he was obliged to speak and act like a grown man. When he was five Barnum taught him to drink wine at dinner with his patrons. At seven he was smoking on the stage. At nine he was chewing tobacco. Later he gave up all of these habits and became a member of the temperance movement.

Although the Thumbs never had a child, midgets can and often do become parents. Frequently the children are of normal size, and it isn't unusual to find a midget father with a young son or daughter towering over him. Because a midget mother is too small to give birth naturally, the baby is delivered by surgery in a caesarean operation. (The operation gets its name from Julius Caesar, who reportedly was born this way.) Lavinia's sister, Minnie, whose husband was short but not a midget, gave birth to a normal-sized baby without a caesarean. She died soon after, and so did the baby.

Tom Thumb kept growing slowly but surely. After he was thirty he reached a height of forty inches (about as tall as a child of five). He became quite heavy, for a midget, weighing as much as seventy pounds. He also grew a beard. Boating was one of his favorite hobbies and he often took part in yacht races—although he needed a man of normal size to handle his boat. In later years he made his home in Middleboro, Massachusetts, where many relics of his life and Lavinia's (including a slice of her wedding cake) may be seen today.

The Thumbs never gave up show business. In 1883 they were touring Wisconsin. One night a fire broke out in their hotel and they could have been burned to death. Luckily their manager rushed to their room and, tucking one of them under each arm, carried them to safety.

For Tom Thumb in particular the fire was a horrifying experience. He never succeeded in putting it out of his mind, and his health began to fail. Six months later, on July 15, 1883, Lavinia came home to find her little husband had died of a stroke.

The general was brought back to Bridgeport for burial in Mountain Grove Cemetery. Ten thousand people, most of them women and girls, came to say good-bye to him. A statue of Tom Thumb was placed in the Stratton family plot, where it can still be seen.

Tom Thumb was only forty-five when he died. Many midgets, however, live as long as ordinary people; his widow, Lavinia, was seventy-eight when she passed away in 1917. Although she had married a second time, she always wore a locket around her neck with a picture of Tom Thumb. At her request she was buried close to her famous first husband.

In Tom Thumb's day no one understood why some of us are born dwarfs. People thought that the mother must have been in an accident or suffered some terrible shock that affected her unborn baby. A short while before Tom Thumb was born his mother's puppy had fallen into a river and drowned. She always felt her grief over the loss of her little pet had caused her son to be born a midget.

General and Mrs. Tom Thumb in later years. The little general grew quite heavy in middle age.

The term "midgets" has traditionally been used for dwarfs whose bodies are perfectly proportioned miniature versions of normal bodies. Their condition can in many cases be traced to their pituitary glands.

The pituitary glands are bean-shaped organs located at the bottom of the skull. They produce a chemical substance called hGH or human growth hormone. If the glands don't make enough hGH a child will be a pituitary dwarf. If they produce too much he may shoot up to a height of seven feet or more—a giant. Both conditions can be caused by heredity.* Fortunately most of us have normal pituitary glands and grow to normal heights.

At birth, pituitary dwarfs may be entirely normal in size, as Tom Thumb was. However, hGH is necessary for growth after birth; lack of it will stunt the child. Even so, pituitary dwarfs grow, many of them to heights greater than Tom Thumb's forty inches.

Much more common than pituitary dwarfs are a second group, chondrodysplastic dwarfs. These people have a number of conditions that affect the bones. Typically they have a normal-sized torso and head, but the arms and legs are usually short and stumpy.** Famous examples are Billy Barty and Herve Villechaize, the movie actors. Some people in this group suffer severely from bony deformities or other problems and need frequent medical attention. Most dwarfism of this kind is also hereditary.

If Tom Thumb had been born in our time his condition might have been corrected. Nowadays injections of growth hormones can help pituitary dwarfs grow taller, sometimes to well over five feet, provided the treatment is begun early enough. To date, doctors have helped several thousand little people in this way.

*Usually only one member of a family has the condition. The Warren sisters were an exception.
**Sometimes these disproportionate dwarfs are mistakenly called "midgets." But midgets are little people who are perfectly proportioned. Both midgets and chondrodysplastic dwarfs are correctly called "dwarfs" or "little people."

Where do the doctors get the hormones for these injections? Curiously enough, they used to obtain them from the pituitary glands of dead bodies donated to medical schools or research institutions. Donated bodies were (and still are) in short supply, and some of them were infected with viruses that could be transmitted with the hormones. Fortunately recent scientific advances have made it possible to manufacture hGH in plentiful amounts by growing it in bacteria.

Since science goes to such great lengths to help little people grow taller, it's ironic that people used to work just as hard to manufacture dwarfs. This was done in ancient Rome, in Europe during the Middle Ages, and in China. In China small children were bought from poor parents and placed in weirdly shaped vases without bottoms. At night the vase was laid on its side so the child could sleep. The child was kept in the vase until he grew to its shape. Then the vase was smashed. "The child comes out," said Victor Hugo, the French author, "and, behold, there is a man in the shape of a mug!"

Since dwarfism is mostly hereditary, groups that marry among themselves are likely to have more dwarf children. One such group is the Amish, a religious sect. There are also some races of people that are small, like the pygmies of Africa. Pygmies aren't dwarfs in the medical sense, since their physical makeup is completely normal.

In a society where everything is made for people of normal size, most little people have a hard time fitting in. Finding a job has been a particularly tough proposition for them.

In earlier centuries kings and noblemen liked to have little people to serve them or to amuse them as jesters. The kings of Spain in particular were fond of dwarfs, and you will see a number of them in the paintings of Velázquez and other artists who worked for the Spanish court.

Many other dwarfs had no choice but to exhibit themselves at fairs or in sideshows and circuses, just as Tom Thumb did. Only in recent times has the situation begun to get better. Today little people hold jobs as accountants, lawyers, doctors, computer programmers, stockbrokers, and in almost every other occupation.

Although the public has come to accept them more and more, dwarfs still face many difficulties ordinary people do not. The emotional problems are often the worst, and they start in early childhood. When normal-sized parents discover their child is not going to grow, they tend to view it as a personal failure and blame themselves because of it. Consciously or unconsciously, they pass their feeling of failure and self-hatred on to the child—who has enough problems of his own without it.

It's easy for the parents of a handicapped child to become overprotective. Because dwarf children need extra help, mothers and fathers may go too far and do too many things for them, so that they come to depend on their parents too much. Actually the children need just the opposite kind of treatment. They need to be trained to stand on their own two feet and to develop confident, strong personalities. Otherwise it will be very hard for them to make their way in a world where almost everyone is bigger than they are.

It sometimes happens that a dwarf child is one of a kind in a town. Because dwarf children are so small or so "different," normal children may be unwilling to play with them, and they may find themselves quite isolated. If loneliness is a problem in childhood it becomes a much more serious one when dwarf children "grow up." Teenagers are often intolerant or clannish and they may refuse to have anything to do with them. Where can they turn to find companionship? And, later, someone to marry? Their experiences can be like that of the dwarf in the old rhyme:

A little man thought he'd look out for a wife.
Said he, "She'll make happy the rest of my life."
He courted a lady—a tall one—who smiled—
"Excuse me," said she, "I took you for a child."

In spite of such difficulties, there are successful marriages between dwarfs and full-sized people—who must, however, face the possibility that their children may also be dwarfs. Naturally marriages of dwarf couples are far commoner.

The little people are a minority, and like other minority groups they have formed an organization to help them deal with their problems. Founded in 1957 by Billy Barty, the dwarf actor, it calls itself Little People of America. Its headquarters is in San Bruno, California, and it has between four and five thousand members.

LPA reaches out in many directions. It works with the average-sized parents of dwarfed children in a number of ways, including support groups, helping them to accept themselves and their children. It provides counseling for teenagers and their special difficulties. Young dwarfs who seek higher education are aided in finding scholarships. Help is provided for little people in financial need.

Every year LPA holds a convention at which members may make new friends and discuss their interests. Average-sized parents attend with their dwarf children, who may for the first time in their lives see other children like themselves and make friends with them. Doctors from major short-stature clinics attend and offer advice and assistance.

One of LPA's important missions is to change the image society has of dwarfs. For centuries people have thought of them in stereotypes—as children, freaks, or subjects for jokes. (Reporters who cover their conventions sometimes cannot resist making fun of them in the articles they write.) Chondrodysplastic dwarfs have a particular grievance; every child is brought up on tales in which dwarfs are pictured as sinister or cruel—when in reality they are the same as anybody else; only their bodies are different.

It's no snap to face life as a little person, knowing that society has stacked the cards against you in a thousand different ways. It takes courage, a giant sense of humor—and the will to see the world as you want it to be. You need to develop the attitude Tom Thumb

Tom Thumb was a particular favorite with children, as this paper doll testifies.

expressed when, as a child, he visited Buckingham Palace and was presented to the three-year-old son of Queen Victoria. The little general placed himself next to the little prince and was dwarfed by him. The difference in sizes, however, didn't get him down.

"The prince is bigger than I am," said the general with a laugh, "but I feel as big as anybody."

Maybe he didn't always, but in public he certainly behaved as if he did. Members of Little People of America seem to have taken his example to heart. Whenever they get together you are sure to hear one of them say, "You're only as big as you feel." They have embodied their philosophy in two little words that they have chosen as their official motto:

THINK BIG

As a schoolboy Robert Wadlow was big enough to toss his father around.

The Tallest Man
in the World

Wherever he went he had to be constantly on the lookout.

On the street, if he wasn't watching, his head might bang against a sign hanging in front of a shop. A lowered awning was always a threat.

Indoors his worries began as he was about to enter an unfamiliar room. He had to take notice of the height of the doorway and make sure he bent low enough. Just a slight miscalculation and he could get a nasty knock on the head.

Once inside, he had to watch out for lighting fixtures hanging from the ceiling. If he didn't, he might bump into a chandelier. Before he sat down in an unfamiliar chair he had to check that it was built solidly enough. A delicately made one could collapse under his enormous weight. His bones were so fragile that even a slight fall could put him in the hospital with a multiple fracture.

He traveled fifty thousand miles a year on business—and every trip had its aggravations. Ordinary train seats didn't give him enough room for his legs, so he had to take a compartment. As he got bigger the compartments got smaller, until they were too small for him to sleep in. Finally his father bought an extra-large automobile that gave him enough space in back for his long legs and a place to stretch out and nap. When his father suggested having the car rebuilt—raising the top so he would have more headroom—he said no. Just as he wanted to be like other people, he wanted the car to look like other cars.

Beds were another problem. If he was to get any sleep he needed one that was longer than he was. Nine feet was the minimum length. At home he had his own special bed, of course. But in hotels two beds had to be set end to end, or one bed had to be placed across the foot of another.

Taking a bath was never comfortable. Bathtubs just weren't made for someone his size. Neither were showers. To shave, he had to stoop to see his face in the mirror. In elevators, too, he had to stoop. As for entering a hotel through a revolving door—impossible.

Sometimes he traveled by airplane. How could a person as big as he was fit into the meager space provided for the average passenger? He needed to buy two seats—the one he sat in and the one in front of it, which had to be taken out so he would have room for his long legs.

His name was Robert Pershing Wadlow and at twenty-two he stood 8 feet 11.1 inches tall in his stocking feet—the tallest man that ever lived, according to medical records.* Great weight goes with great height; at his peak he weighed 491 pounds. His hands measured twelve and three-quarter inches from the wrist to the tip of his middle finger. His feet were enormous. He wore a size 37AA—the biggest pair of shoes ever made to fit a human being. (It took five square feet of leather to make them.)

Robert was born on February 22, 1918, in Alton, Illinois, a railroad center not far from Chicago. At birth he was a good-sized baby, weighing eight and a half pounds. He appeared so normal that

---

The title of the tallest man that ever lived has been claimed by or for many, including Cajanus (1714–49) of Finland. Cajanus was reported to be 9 feet 3.4 inches tall. Measurement of his right femur, in a Dutch museum, shows he probably stood 7 feet 3.4 inches. Wadlow's claim is the only one with scientific backing.

nobody bothered to make a note of his height.

At six months the lovely, round-faced, blond baby boy tipped the scales at thirty pounds—twice as heavy as many children that age, but not so heavy as to cause worry. By eighteen months, however, his weight had shot up to sixty-two pounds and his parents had trouble carrying him. They seem to have kept no record of his height; perhaps they expected his growth would soon slow down.

But it didn't. When the boy was three his mother and father went on a train trip with him. They didn't buy him a ticket; he was too young to need one. The conductor thought otherwise. To him the boy looked over five and he told the Wadlows they had to purchase a ticket for him. Mr. Wadlow was obliged to give in. After that, to avoid embarrassment, they always bought a ticket for their son even though he was underage.

When Robert was five his father decided to take out an insurance policy on his life. The boy received a physical examination and the doctor noted his height and weight: five feet four inches, 105 pounds. The insurance company returned the application, saying there had to be some mistake; no child of five could be that big. The doctor certified the figures were correct and Robert got his policy.

In 1923, at five and a half, the boy entered grade school. The teacher and her other pupils stared at him in disbelief. Dressed in a suit that would fit a seventeen year old, he looked more like an adult than a child.

It didn't take them long to discover that, in spite of appearances, at heart and at head he was a child just like the rest. He loved the same games, laughed at the same jokes, and had the same trouble learning his ABCs. There was one significant difference. When he played some strenuous game he tired more easily than the others, and sometimes he said his legs hurt. The reason would become clearer with time: his rapid growth kept using up the calcium in his body, weakening the bones in his legs, which had to bear his ever-increasing weight.

At eight Robert went into the third grade. He was a six-footer now, weighing 169 pounds. The seats in the classroom were too small for him and a full-sized chair had to be brought in. He couldn't sit at his desk until big wooden blocks were placed under its legs. He was an odd sight, bending over to take a drink from a water fountain made for children or standing with his classmates like Gulliver the Man-Mountain among the tiny people of Lilliput. But no matter how uncomfortable or out of place he felt, he studied hard and he earned good grades. He had a high IQ.

It didn't take the news media long to learn about the young giant. Once they had discovered Robert they never left him in peace. Photographs of the boy, with accounts of his phenomenal growth, appeared in newspapers all over the United States. News films (called newsreels) were a popular feature in movie theaters in the 1920s. Through them his face and figure became known to millions. A name was coined for him: the Alton Giant.

Each new birthday brought a crowd of reporters to the Wadlow doorstep, hungry for the latest about the boy's growth, his health, his hobbies. Magazine feature writers, doctors, advertising men, and ordinary busybodies were always ringing the Wadlows' bell; they became a constant nuisance to a family that wanted only to live its own life. For Robert, who wished more than anything else to be a boy like any other, it was a reminder that he wasn't—and never would be.

In 1927, only a child of nine, he was six feet two and a half inches tall. A photograph taken that year shows him standing next to his father. The older Wadlow appears serious, if not worried. (He often looked worried in pictures taken with his son.) Robert's face, by contrast, has the smooth, pleasant look of a good-natured child. Of the two, the son is the taller. (*Time* magazine wrote at this time that he was able to toss his father around.) His clothing bill must have been substantial, for he outgrew his garments soon after they were bought. For a while his castoffs, almost new, had been passed on to his father.

Not his shoes, however. His feet were much too big for ordinary store-bought shoes. His had to be made to order on a special last that needed to be replaced regularly. It took a long time to get the shoes from the manufacturer; by the time they were delivered, sometimes he had already outgrown them. And the bigger they were, the more they cost.

At eleven Robert was six feet seven inches tall. His rate of growth attracted the attention of doctors at Barnes Hospital in nearby St. Louis and they invited his father to bring him in for an examination. The older Wadlow quickly agreed. He and his wife were greatly worried about their giant son. They had many questions they wanted to ask the doctors. The two most important were: Why was he growing so fast—and what could be done about it?

As soon as the specialists at Barnes looked at Robert they knew what his trouble was. His pituitary glands were overactive. These tiny glands, as we saw in the last chapter, manufacture hGH—growth hormones. A normal quantity of hGH produces a human being of normal size. But Robert's glands were overactive. Because of some abnormality—most likely a tumor on the glands—they were secreting excessive amounts of growth hormone. As a result the long bones of his body were growing at an unusual rate. And there was no telling when the growth would stop.

The boy, the doctors explained, was a pathological giant—his giantism was caused by disease. The outlook for him wasn't especially good. His rapid growth could lead to many serious physical problems (not to mention mental ones). Pituitary giants often didn't live beyond their twenties.*

Not much can be more painful for parents than to hear that

---

*Medically speaking, only a pathological giant is a true giant. In popular terms, however, any man taller than 6 feet 6.7 inches is a giant. (A woman must be at least 6 feet 1.6 inches tall.) Completely normal people can be as tall as that or taller. Height is usually genetically programmed (hereditary); tall parents are likely to have tall children. Tallness can also be racial. The Watusi people of Africa, who are well known for their height, may grow to seven feet or more.

their child may face disease and early death. The Wadlows felt desperate. Wasn't there some operation that could help their boy, they asked.

There wasn't. Science, they were informed, knew very little about the pituitary glands. In some cases like Robert's, operations had been performed and a portion of the pituitaries removed. But the surgery was risky; instead of curing, it might kill. Don't permit such an operation to be performed on your son, the doctors strongly advised.*

The staff at Barnes Hospital were to get to know Robert very well. Every year his father brought him back for examination. Every year he submitted without complaining to one test after another, although some were extremely painful. Always his parents held on to the hope that the doctors might discover something that would help him. In the same hope the boy stood uncomfortably in front of the curious, probing eyes of students at Washington University Medical School, an affiliate of Barnes, and listened as the professors lectured about him. Later on he would suffer from leg infections and return to Barnes for treatment.

His growth was ceaseless. In 1930 he reached seven feet. He was only twelve and in his first year of junior high school. At church, in school, wherever he went, no one could fail to see him; he stood head and shoulders over everybody around. A celebrity in spite of himself, he was constantly invited to make appearances.

That year Robert's father received an unusual proposition. The Peters Shoe Company of St. Louis offered to supply the boy with all the shoes he needed and to pay him as well. In exchange it wanted him to act in a movie promoting its line of children's shoes. He wouldn't need any special acting skills—he'd just be himself, doing

Today the advice would be different. Knowledge of the pituitary glands and surgical techniques have both advanced considerably since the 1920s. Successful operations are performed nowadays for the removal of a tumor of the pituitaries, or the tumor may be irradiated, so a pathological giant will stop growing.

the things he did every day, while a camera crew followed him around and filmed him. The film would then be shown in movie theaters and Robert would make personal appearances in connection with it. Later he'd also be asked to appear in stores selling the company's products.

It was a proposition the Wadlows could hardly say no to. The boy's extraordinary size was making it almost impossible to buy ready-made clothing for him anymore. Almost everything he wore had to be made to order, which was very expensive. With the family getting larger, Robert's free shoes and his earnings would be a big help.

The following year he turned thirteen. It was a birthday he'd been looking forward to. Raising his right hand, he took the Boy Scout oath—becoming, at seven feet three inches, the tallest scout in the entire world.

Boy Scouts do a lot of things. With his enormous height and weight (260 pounds), he couldn't do everything the others did. But he tried hard. He loved especially to go on long hikes. His long strides gave him an advantage here, but he shortened them; walking with his friends was more important than being in the lead. When he got home his calcium-poor legs often ached.

The game of leapfrog provided him and his fellow scouts with many laughs. With the members of the troop bent over, he simply walked along and spread his legs apart to pass over each boy. When their turn came they leapfrogged over each other—until, reaching their tall friend, they stooped and walked between his great outspread legs. At a Boy Scout camp he posed proudly in his smart new uniform—tailor-made, naturally—while newsreel cameras whirred.

In 1932 the boy entered high school. By now he had two sisters and a brother, all of normal height. He, by contrast, stood more than seven and a half feet tall and weighed more than three hundred pounds. The older of his sisters, when she walked with him, had once been able to hold his hand. Now she couldn't even reach it. His mother, by standing on her toes, had once been able to touch his shoulder. No more. But Robert, looming over her, could easily rest his hand on top of her shoulder.

He reached his sixteenth birthday in 1934. He had also reached a height of seven feet ten inches—and he was still shooting upward. If you had searched all over North America you wouldn't have found anybody taller than he was. His weight was close to four hundred pounds.

As Robert got bigger, everything in the world was shrinking. Knives and forks were like a child's toys in his gigantic hands. The buttons on his clothes seemed to be made for Lilliputian fingers. When he sat down to eat with his family, finding a comfortable position for his great legs took effort. His feet were so huge he had to be extremely watchful going up and down stairs. He couldn't write on the blackboard in school without stooping.

In spite of his physical difficulties nobody heard him complain. It was almost as if he'd made up his mind his handicap wouldn't get the upper hand; instead, he would try to use it to his advantage. His height quickly won him respect on the basketball court. Loping up to the basket, he simply had to reach up and drop the ball in. Unfortunately he couldn't play the game for long; the strain on his legs became too painful.

In 1935, when Robert was seventeen—he was already more than eight feet tall—a dangerous case of influenza laid him on his back. At the same time he had a serious infection in his foot. He was running a high fever and the doctor ordered him into the hospital. An ambulance clanged up to the Wadlow house but the stretcher bearers saw at once he was too much for them. Eight men had to be rounded up to carry the giant downstairs and place him in the ambulance.

For days the boy burned with fever. He teetered between life and death. His weight dropped sixty pounds. In the end he recovered. But it was only too clear his pituitary condition was taking its toll. Although he was only seventeen, he had developed arthritis. Sometime earlier, too, he had injured the metatarsal bones in his foot. Both problems would stay with him the rest of his life.

In 1936 the giant finished high school in the upper half of his

Still growing. Robert with his father a few years after the previous picture was taken. His autograph is at lower right.

class. No graduation gown could be found big enough for some-body eight feet three inches tall. One had to be specially made, and it took fourteen yards of cloth. The principal of Alton High posed for a photograph with the school's tallest graduate. The top of the man's head just reached the boy's elbow.

Robert had been thinking about his future; he decided he wanted to become a lawyer. Several colleges, including some out of town, had offered him four-year scholarships. He chose Shurtleff College, right in Alton, for he didn't want to leave his family.

College brought new difficulties. For example, to reach Shurtleff Robert had to take a taxi. Just getting his great body in and out of the back seat of the little cab was a feat in human engineering. The professors gave lectures, and some spoke so rapidly it was hard even for a normal person to take notes fast enough; for Robert, grasping a tiny fountain pen in his huge hand, it was impossible. Desks and seats were too small. In the science laboratory he needed more time than anyone else to make the necessary delicate adjustments on his microscope or to dissect tiny specimens. He missed the old, familiar faces of high school; many of the students now were strangers, and some gaped at him or whispered behind his back.

The worst time for him was the winter. Classes were held in different buildings, sometimes a block or two apart, and the streets were buried under ice and snow. His height and weight made him awkward, and the possibility of a fall was always present. It was always frightening too, because a slight fall could mean a severe injury. To get from one class to another he needed to ask two students to help him. Standing between them, he would take a firm grip on their shoulders and step cautiously forward. It was hard to arrive on time.

During his first year at Shurtleff the boy began to doubt the wisdom of his choice of a career. He also doubted he would be able to finish college. By the end of the summer vacation he had changed his plans. From his work for the shoe company he knew he could

When the giant pruned a tree he had no need of a ladder.

attract people into shoe stores. Why not go into business for himself and open his own store? In time he might own a string of shops and make a good living. He could still continue his education by attending school at night.

So far Robert had worked for the shoe people just during vacations and weekends. Now he unveiled a new program to his father: he wanted to work full time so he could raise the funds he'd need to set himself up in business. Besides working for the shoe company he could do other things, like making personal appearances for organizations and running a soft-drink stand at the Illinois State Fair. He'd need a manager, though—and no one could handle that job better than his own father. The idea made good sense to the older Wadlow. He resigned his engineering position and went into partnership with his son.

The following year the giant turned nineteen. At eight feet five inches he was taller than anyone who ever lived of whom we have an authentic record. He wasn't the heaviest person,* though—he only weighed a meager four hundred and eighty pounds!

On Robert's birthday, as usual, reporters poured into the Wadlow home to take pictures and get his latest statistics. One newsman commented: "For as long as he can remember, people have stared at him; he has been *different* from others.

"Nineteen is an age at which most boys and girls long passionately to conform, to be and to do exactly as others in the same group are and do. At nineteen Robert Wadlow, because of his gigantic frame, cannot do many of the things they do.

"You might expect a boy in that situation to be bitter and sullen, but Robert Wadlow isn't. At his Alton home he told an *Evening American* reporter the other day:

" 'I have got used to being stared at. To resent it would only make folks unhappy, including myself. Some people say unkind

That title apparently belongs to Jon Brower Minnoch (1941–83), who reportedly weighed fourteen hundred pounds.

things, of course. I thought it over long ago and decided to ignore them. The worst you can say about them is that they are thoughtless.' "

Robert could no longer get about on his weak legs without leaning on a cane. But get about he did, traveling with his father from state to state and making appearances at shoe stores, conventions, and public events, where he was a featured guest introduced by important government officials.

That year an invitation came from the Ringling Brothers and Barnum & Bailey Circus. The Tallest Man in the World could be a powerful drawing card, and they wanted to feature him when they performed in New York City and Boston.

Life as a circus performer has attracted countless people, especially human oddities, who often have had no other way to earn their livelihood. It didn't hold any special charm for Robert, though; he had turned down offers like this one before. But now, when the circus promised he wouldn't have to appear in the sideshow but would be treated as a star, he decided to accept. Why not? The pay was excellent, he would stay with his father in the best hotels, all of their expenses would be paid—and it would bring his shoe store closer.

Ringling Brothers opened in New York City's Madison Square Garden. Robert had always objected when photographers got in front of him to take pictures from a low angle to exaggerate his height. Now he turned down a circus request that he wear a full-dress suit as well as a high hat and high-heeled shoes that would make him look even taller than he was. He insisted on being himself, and he appeared in an everyday business suit. Standing under the spotlights in one of the circus's three rings—the other two were empty and dark—he was greeted with waves of applause. He remained in the ring just a few minutes while his story was told and then he bowed and left. He made only two appearances a day. During the time the circus featured him it broke all its attendance records.

The Tallest Man in the World with some friends from the Ringling Brothers Circus. Note that he has outgrown his jacket.

For the young giant from the Midwest, visiting New York City offered a rare opportunity: he could see all the famous sights he'd been hearing and reading about all his life. He saw them—and he was fussed over wherever he went and pursued by the press. At the Empire State Building he was greeted by Al Smith, former governor of the state. At the New York Stock Exchange hundreds and hundreds of brokers who were buying and selling frantically on the floor halted business and gave him an ovation. He was a popular guest on radio shows, including Ripley's "Believe It Or Not." In Boston he shook hands with Admiral Richard E. Byrd, who had made the first flight over the South Pole.

Getting ready to fly back home, Robert had a curious mishap. While he was taking his seat in the airplane one of his elbows struck the window and cracked it. The plane was no longer fit to fly. Another had to be brought in and all the baggage transferred to it before the flight could begin.

Although he was a celebrity, Robert was still the same home-loving, gentle, unspoiled boy he had always been. When he wasn't on tour nothing gave him so much pleasure as spending time with his family and helping around the house. Great height, he found, could come in handy in doing many household chores. Window washing was one—the young giant could wash the windows on the outside of the house without standing on a ladder. Inside, with his feet on the floor, he could clean the top shelves of cabinets or hang curtains. Wiping the kitchen ceiling was a snap—it was just inches over his head.

He had many friends in Alton, including girls. To one he became deeply attached, but he lost her; his size seemed to make that inevitable. However, he received plenty of warmth and affection from his family. A new baby brother came to play a big part in his life. He loved to rock the baby to sleep and, later on, enjoyed having the child climb all over him. On his trips he took delight in picking up little children and cuddling them. Whenever he got home from a tour his suitcase was packed with presents he'd bought for his

Great height is a distinct advantage in washing windows.

mother, his brothers, and his sisters.

In the next few years the giant traveled to hundreds and hundreds of cities with his father and an assistant. The stores where he appeared were always swamped with crowds; lengthy lines had to wait outside a long time to get in and see him.

After a time he came up with a bright solution to the problem. A platform was erected in front of the store or, when that wasn't possible, a big truck with an open back was parked there. Standing on the platform or the truck back, his tall figure was visible to everyone. He brought along his own public address equipment so he could be heard as well. Besides promoting the shoe company's products, father and son kept the crowds in stitches with their jokes, and they answered their questions. Sometimes the spectators numbered as many as fifteen or twenty thousand.

At his public appearances the boy was sometimes baited by people who insisted he couldn't possibly be as tall as he was said to be. Some asserted he wasn't a giant at all—he was standing on stilts inside his long trousers.

In Arkansas, once, Robert found a bigger crowd than usual waiting. They had a giant of their own in town and were betting he was taller than young Wadlow. To show his height the Arkansas giant climbed up on the platform and stood next to the giant from Alton. Which man was taller? Anyone who had eyes could see—but to clinch the matter Robert stretched out his arm. The Arkansas giant's hair didn't even touch it.

Sometimes, to amuse the onlookers, Robert would put a silver dollar on top of his head. Any person able to take the coin off, he announced, could keep it. Although many tried, nobody under six feet ten inches ever walked away with it.

Because a person is very big, people suppose he must have a gigantic appetite. This certainly wasn't true of the young man from Alton. In 1938 an article in *Time* magazine asserted he had a dozen eggs for breakfast. Other articles said he ate four times as much as the average person. His father disagreed. He estimated his son ate about ten percent more than the average person. The public was always enormously curious about his eating; when he dined in a restaurant many eyes followed every spoonful of food he put in his mouth.

In 1938 Robert's tour took him along the West Coast. In Hollywood he visited the movie studios. He was an enthusiastic collector of autographs and here was an opportunity to get some really great ones. At the Metro-Goldwyn-Mayer Studios he posed for a photograph with Maureen O'Sullivan, young costar of the Tarzan movies, while she wrote in his album. The top of her head barely reached his waist.

On the way north the Wadlows drove through a forest of redwoods. Getting out of the car, they walked among the lofty trees, the tallest and oldest in America. Robert stopped next to one and his eyes traveled up its trunk, hundreds of feet high. He placed one hand against it.

"Dad," he said, and his father heard an unusual quaver in his deep voice, "this is the first time in my life I ever felt small." He paused. "I like it." He paused again. "I *like* it."

In 1939 he celebrated his twenty-first birthday. He now stood eight feet eight and one-quarter inches tall; his weight was 491 pounds. It was to be a big year for the big man. He had reached voting age, and he took a great interest in politics; he could hardly wait to cast his first ballot.

The voting booth, like most other things, wasn't made for a giant. Raising the canvas curtain and bending very low, he managed to get inside. The voting table (this was before the days of electronic voting machines) was much too low for him to write on. With his hat brushing the ceiling, he held the ballot high up against the wall and checked off his choices. It was supposed to be a secret ballot but anyone could see how he voted.

That year Robert's travels took him west again. In one Minnesota town Indian chiefs, dressed in colorful ceremonial costumes, chanted solemnly and adopted him as a member of their tribe. They

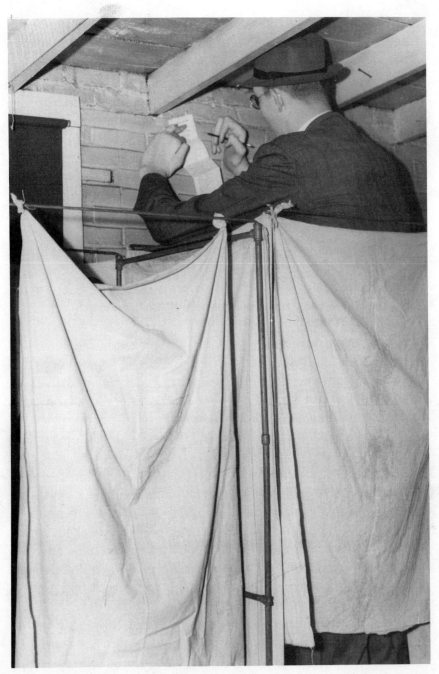

Voting booths are not made for giants.

also gave him a name in their language: Tall Pine.

On the giant's twenty-second birthday, in 1940, he stood an astonishing 8 feet 11.1 inches tall. His schedule called for him to take part in a festival and parade in Manistee, Wisconsin, on July 4. At lunch that day he wasn't feeling well and he was unable to eat a bite. His father was worried.

The parade was slow in getting started. Finally it began to wind through the town. In the giant's car the older Wadlow saw that Robert was looking sicker by the minute; he could barely sit up. His father decided they would have to leave the parade as quickly as possible. But when they tried, all the streets were jammed. It was hours before they were able to get to their hotel.

One bed was quickly pushed crosswise against the foot of the other, and the ailing giant collapsed on them. The house physician was called.

Robert was running a high fever. To support his ankle he had recently been fitted with a new brace, but the fit wasn't very good and his skin had been broken. An infection had developed; because sensation in his feet was limited, he hadn't been aware of any pain.

The physician said a hospital was the only proper place for Robert. But the giant remembered all the trouble that moving him to one had caused five years before. He refused to go.

Three more doctors were called in and consulted together. Barnes Hospital in St. Louis was telephoned for advice. X-rays were taken. No treatment seemed to help.* His mother was sent for.

Robert was critically ill. He couldn't eat and he kept losing weight. From time to time his position in the bed had to be changed but he was too weak even to move by himself. To shift the giant's helpless, heavy body required the combined strength of the nurse and his father and mother.

His condition grew worse. On the night of July 14 he was in

Antibiotics might have helped to control his infection but they did not become available until later, during World War II.

His head almost touching the ceiling, Robert poses with his two brothers.

extreme pain. The doctor had to give him a drug to relieve his suffering and help him fall asleep. He had been very upset, but not because of his illness. The doctor had told him he wouldn't be well enough to go to his grandparents' golden wedding anniversary celebration in Alton—and he had been looking forward to it for months.

Exhausted with watching and worrying, his unhappy mother and father finally lay down to rest. Early in the morning of July 15 they heard someone slip into their room. It was Robert's nurse. One look at her pale, drawn face and they knew why she had come.

A giant's burial requires a giant's coffin. Robert's had to be specially made in a hurry; it was ten feet long and thirty-two inches wide inside.

News of the death of the world's tallest man flashed across the country, and great numbers of people flocked to the funeral home in Alton, some from considerable distances. Many who had waited in line to see the friendly giant when he visited their hometowns now stood in line all night long to get inside and say good-bye to him. When the doors were finally closed forty-six thousand people had viewed the body; thousands more couldn't be admitted.

Robert's coffin was too big to be carried into the church, so services were held at the funeral home. Businesses and city offices closed down to honor Alton's most famous son, and flags hung at half mast. Boy Scouts were drafted to help the local police and state troopers direct the heavy traffic as thousands drove to the cemetery to see him buried.

For hundreds of years physicians and anatomical museums have collected the remains of giants and other human oddities and exhibited them. Robert had read some ghoulish stories that told how body snatchers had stolen the bodies of dead giants*—stories

*The two most notable were Charlie Byrne and Cornelius Magrath, both pituitary giants who died in their early twenties like Robert. Their stories are related in the author's book Body Snatchers, Stiffs and Other Ghoulish Delights (Fawcett/Ballantine, 1987).

that had made his blood run cold. More than once he had asked his father to make sure nothing of the kind would ever happen to him.

When the young giant was laid to rest, his massive casket was sealed inside a thick protective casing of reinforced concrete. No ghoul would ever trouble his long, long sleep.

Julia Pastrana in a rare daguerreotype. Often advertised as a hybrid—a cross between an ape and a human being—she was actually a bearded Mexican Indian woman.

Apewoman

She pirouetted onto the stage, her red skirt swirling, and stopped just behind the footlights. Perhaps her manager had told her to do that so the audience could get a good close-up look at her.

They did. In the front rows there were loud gasps. One woman screamed. Another slumped fainting in her seat.

They had come to the theater expecting to see a great curiosity—a creature not entirely human. They had read she was a hybrid—a cross between a human being and an ape.

Now, staring at the incredible figure poised before them, they could believe it.

She was a dwarf, no more than four and a half feet tall. Her colorful embroidered skirt reached just below her knees, exposing bare legs covered with hair, like an ape's. Amid the hair on her throat a necklace glittered. Her arms and shoulders were dark with hair.

Nothing about her was more apelike than her head. Hair covered much of her face, lustrous black hair, dense in some places, thinner in others. On her forehead the hair was short and fine, but at the eyebrows it became a black mass so thick and heavy it overhung her dark eyes like a visor.

Hair ran down her cheeks in luxuriant sideburns. They broadened until they came together on her chin to form a grotesque beard. It must have been five or six inches long. Hair reached across her upper lip in a mustache. Dense hair clothed her ears, almost hiding them. Long tufts hung from the lobes.

Her nose was broad and bulbous. Hair grew on it. Hair grew out of it, making her huge nostrils huger.

But her mouth! The jaws thrust forward from her face like the protruding jaws of a gorilla. Her lips, so thick they looked swollen, were two or three times the size of normal lips. When she parted them in a shy smile you could see enormous red gums and a hint of curious, malformed teeth.

She had the head of a gargoyle but her form was very much the form of a woman. Her bosom was full, her waist was narrow. Her arms and legs had a womanly roundness and her hands and feet were delicate and small. Her eyes, large and black, were intensely human. She looked as if she might burst into tears at any moment.

She nodded to her accompanist and a lively Mexican tune rang through the hall. Hands high over her head, she spun about. Castanets clicked. Pitching her body backward at the waist, she thrust each leg out in turn before her in the slow, deliberate rhythm of a gypsy dance. Her heels stamped so hard the hollow stage echoed.

Abruptly the music stopped. The dancer stopped with it, hands frozen over her head, still as a statue. Abruptly the music started up again. The frozen figure came instantly to life. The music grew louder and louder, faster and faster. Her arms and legs became blurs in the air as, eyes shining, she whirled about, a leaf spinning in the wind. When the music died she curtseyed and bowed deeply.

The applause was stormy, wave upon wave of it. Apewoman she may be, the audience seemed to be saying, but she can dance!

And now she was singing. Sometimes she sang in Spanish, sometimes in English with a heavy Mexican accent. People leaned forward, wondering. How could a voice so tender and sweet come from such a hairy monster? Hands clapped long and hard. She bowed again and again. But now the sad, hurt look had vanished from her eyes and she was smiling happily.

Julia Pastrana's performances at Horticultural Hall in Boston in September 1855 were a considerable success. They were far from her first. In one city after another, this creature with the grace of a ballerina, the voice of an angel, and the face of an ape had been evoking both horror and delight in thousands.

Julia's career was a spectacular one. It started in 1854, when she first stepped out on a stage in the United States. Her fame—or her notoriety—blazed across two continents with her. Today, more than a hundred years after her death, people still know her name.

Who—or what—was Julia?

An excellent dancer, Julia usually wore costumes that left her arms and shoulders (and often her legs) bare so people could see how hairy she was. She loved to decorate her hair with ribbons, beads, and flowers.

Her origins are shrouded in mystery. The first account we have of her early life was published in 1855, in Boston. It bore this lurid title: *HYBRID INDIAN! The Misnomered Bear Woman, Julia Pastrana.* Very likely it was sold at her performances, perhaps by Julia herself. Adorning the cover was a picture of her, hairy face and all, in a fashionable gown of the period, frilled pantaloons peeping out below a wide skirt.

Julia, the pamphlet related, was born into a tribe of Indians living in the Sierra Madre of the state of Sinaloa, on the west coast of Mexico, near the Gulf of California.

Her tribe was "semi-human."

"They live in caves, in a naked state," the pamphlet declared, "and subsist on grass, roots, bark of trees, etc., they eat no animal food! . . . Their face and whole person is covered with a thick, black hair, and their features have a close resemblance to those of a Bear and Orang Outang. Their mouths are elongated with very thick double lips; they have no upper front teeth. . . . They have intellect, and are endowed with speech. . . . They have always been looked upon by travellers as a kind of link between the man and the brute creation."

No tribe of Indians answering to this physical description is known anywhere. Probably it was made up to account for Julia's peculiar appearance. But there once were in the West, including the state of Sinaloa, Indians with just such a primitive lifestyle. Usually they lived in areas so desolate and arid it was impossible to grow any kind of crop. Unfriendly whites—and most whites were unfriendly—sometimes called them "Root Diggers" or, simply, "Digger Indians."

Nestled at the edge of the mountains where this tribe lived was a little Mexican town, Copala. Some of its women used to go up to bathe in a pond on the mountainside. One day, when they got home, they suddenly realized one of the women who had gone up with them, a Mrs. Espinosa, was missing. A search party was sent out but could not find her anywhere. She must have drowned, they decided, and returned home.

Six years passed. On the mountainside above Copala one day, a *ranchero* was searching for some cattle that had strayed. Passing near a cave, he heard a voice. He recognized at once that it belonged to a Mexican woman. Afraid to venture into the cave by himself, he hurried down to Copala for help. A party of armed men was organized and, coming back to the cave, they surrounded it. By a clever trick they managed to rescue the woman from the Indians. She turned out to be the long-missing Mrs. Espinosa.

With her Mrs. Espinosa brought a little Indian girl. The woman explained that she had been captured by the mountain tribe, who took her to live with them in the cave. (Such happenings were not unknown. Whites were often captured by Indians and adopted by them. Many intermarried with the Indians and spent the rest of their lives with them.)

While she was living with the mountain tribe, Mrs. Espinosa related, an Indian woman died soon after giving birth to a daughter. The Indians gave the baby to Mrs. Espinosa to take care of. The Mexican woman came to love the child and could not bear to leave her behind when she was rescued. In Copala, with Mr. and Mrs. Espinosa as her godparents, the child was baptized Julia Pastrana.

According to the pamphlet, some years later the Espinosas left Copala. They did not take the girl with them, but left her in the care of Pedro Sanchez, governor of the State of Sinaloa. Perhaps, like some other hairy children, she already had a small beard; she could have been an object of interest and amusement to the governor and his family. She worked as a servant for them.

"She remained in the family until April, 1854," we are told, "when, finding no happiness here in consequence of their bad treatment, she left home, resolved to go to the mountains again." She was about twenty-two at this time. In the woods near Copala she met a man named Rates. Looking at the strange hairy girl, he realized that here was a sight people would pay to see. He persuaded her to come to the United States to be exhibited, no doubt telling her he would make her rich.

Accompanied by Rates and another man, Julia arrived in New Orleans in October 1854. From there they headed directly for New York City.

Interest in human oddities like Julia was at a peak in the 1850s. P. T. Barnum hadn't started the trend, but he certainly helped to bring it to new heights. In 1835 he had exhibited Joice Heth, who he said had been George Washington's nursemaid and was 161 years old. (At her death an autopsy showed she was about eighty years younger.) He had won a wide reputation with his Feejee Mermaid; advertisements of her beauty lured thousands into his American Museum. Inside, they gaped at a hideous eighteen-inch-long creature that was actually half a monkey, half a fish, and all dead. Among his other sensations were General Tom Thumb, Jr.; Vantile Mack, the Giant Baby, said to weigh 257 pounds; and a host of others. Only a year before Julia came to town, New Yorkers had been treated to the sight of Madame Joseph Clofullia, the Swiss bearded lady, and her bearded little son. Every few weeks brought a new human oddity to the city. The new one now—and certainly the oddest in years—was Julia Pastrana.

Julia quickly attracted attention. "The eyes of this *lusus naturae* [sport of nature]," wrote one reporter, "beam with intelligence, while its jaws, jagged fangs and ears are terrifically hideous. . . . Nearly its whole frame is coated with long glossy hair. Its voice is harmonious, for this semi-human being is perfectly docile, and speaks the Spanish language." Like other human oddities, she answered questions from the audience; she, however, needed the help of her manager.

Early in her New York stay Julia was taken to be examined by a physician. Showmen often used to have their human oddities undergo a medical examination to prove they were genuine. P. T. Barnum, when he exhibited Madame Clofullia, was sued for fraud by a man who insisted that only males had beards. Barnum produced testimonials from doctors certifying they had examined Clofullia and she was an authentic woman. Now, in his turn, Julia's exhibitor obtained a testimonial signed by a physician. It stated:

"She is a perfect woman—a rational creature, endowed with speech, which no monster has ever possessed. She is therefore a HYBRID, wherein the nature of a woman predominates over the brute—the Orang Outang. Altogether she is one of the most extraordinary beings of the present day." It was signed "Alex B. Mott, M.D."

How would Julia have felt if she could have read Dr. Mott's certificate? Hairy and ape faced, she knew how different she was from other people—they would never let her forget that—and if she ever happened to, one look in the mirror would give her a sharp reminder. If she ever ventured out of doors without covering her face with a heavy veil a crowd of curiosity seekers would gather and follow her through the streets. Burdened by her own strangeness, she might well have believed the doctor's statement.

Julia Pastrana was of course no hybrid. A hybrid is the offspring of two different but related species, such as a horse and a donkey (the offspring is a mule). A true hybrid, like the mule, cannot reproduce. Julia, we shall see, could.

Physically Julia was different from other people in three ways. The first was her shortness. The cause could have been glandular, as in Tom Thumb. But that is highly unlikely, since her shortness wasn't extreme. Hers was a type that often runs in families. It might also be expected to occur in a tribe of Indians who are isolated and marry only within their own group.

Julia's second difference was her extreme hairiness. This condition, known scientifically as hirsutism, is usually due to a disorder of the endocrine glands.

In Julia's case the glands at fault could have been the ovaries. These glands, besides producing eggs and female sex hormones, secrete small amounts of male sex hormones. Sometimes a tumor or other abnormality may make the ovaries produce too much of these male hormones. When this happens a woman can have a beard and excessive hair in other parts of the body. A disorder of the adrenal or pituitary glands may also cause extreme hairiness. Nowadays these problems are helped by administering hormones or other treatment. All of this was unknown in Julia's time.

Julia's third difference involved her gums and teeth. Her gums were exceptionally thick and heavy. (Dentists call this condition gingival hyperplasia.) The enlarged gums pushed her lips and the area around them outward, giving her an apelike appearance. The cause could have been scurvy, resulting from a diet lacking in vitamin C.

Descriptions of Julia's teeth differ, but all agree they were abnormal. It seems likely she had a complete set of teeth in the lower jaw. In the upper jaw only her back teeth (molars) were fully developed; the front teeth were undeveloped or malformed. The cause was probably genetic and linked to her hairiness.

Julia's tour took her around the country. In February she was back in New Orleans. When August came she was in the Midwest, appearing in showplaces in Ohio. Because her skin was dark—according to some reports a yellowish brown—the word must have gotten about that she was a black, and not a hybrid, as her manager advertised. To settle this rumor (and no doubt get more publicity) her manager took her for an examination to the office of Dr. S. Brainerd in Cleveland. Brainerd made a simple test. He placed one of Julia's hairs next to that of an "African" under a powerful magnifying lens and compared them. "The individual in question," he certified, "possesses by this test no trace of NEGRO BLOOD."

Professor Brainerd examined her further. "Her other peculiarities," he went on, "the hair upon the body, its length and structure, the form of the mouth and nose, the size of her limbs, peculiarity of her breasts, etc., and various other features, entitle her, I think, to the rank of a distinct species." Anthropology in the 1850s still had a long way to go.

In September Julia was in Boston, performing, we saw earlier, at the Horticultural Hall. Her manager, now a Mr. Beach, must have decided to get a more expert opinion about her. Taking her to the Boston Society of Natural History, he consulted its curator of comparative anatomy, Samuel Kneeland, Jr.

As a comparative anatomist, Kneeland was better qualified to judge Julia's place in the animal kingdom than any of the doctors who had examined her. His opinion was unhesitating. "She is a perfect woman. . . . She is certainly human." She was in no way a black,* he declared, but belonged to an Indian tribe.

The lot of a traveling entertainer is rarely easy. Julia, speaking little English, knowing nobody, and completely dependent on her manager, had to do whatever was asked of her. Her day was a long one. Her first performance began at ten A.M., her last ended at nine P.M. In between she had a few hours to rest and take her meals. Life was rushed and hectic—and lonesome. If she had stayed in a town or at a fair for a while she might have had a chance to make a friend or two. But she was always on the move and her friendships were necessarily few and brief. Letters might have helped to keep them alive but she didn't know how to read and write.

For two years Julia toured the United States. She was also taken on tour in Canada. Her managers changed. In the summer of 1857 her latest, a man named Lent, took her to Europe.

In July Julia opened in London at the Regent Gallery. Journalists were invited by Lent to a private show and they liked what they saw and heard. Julia's English was much better now. She answered their questions without hesitation and they were struck by her excellent sense of humor. Holding a rose with a long stem, she sang "The Last Rose of Summer" in a way that moved them. Lent told the journalists she was a wild girl he had found living alone with wild animals in Central America. Her beard, her hairy body, and her

---

*The myth that Julia was a black or part ape is still alive. Not long ago the author received a racist leaflet printed in the South with a picture of Julia Pastrana. The heading read: "Result of Mating of Ape with Negro Woman."

grotesque face may have persuaded some he was telling the truth. But Julia did not behave like a wild girl, and her lovely voice and graceful dancing were much admired.

The important British medical journal *Lancet,* always interested in human oddities, sent a man to report on Miss Pastrana. He commented on her abnormally heavy gums and how her lips protruded. In her upper jaw, he said, "the front teeth are all but deficient, the molars alone being properly developed." Nothing about her lower teeth appeared abnormal. Her nostrils, he observed, "are remarkably flattened and expanded, and so soft as to seem destitute of cartilage."

He found her hairiness striking. "Indeed, the whole of the body, excepting the palms of the hands and the soles of the feet, is more or less clothed with hair." Yet he never questioned that she was a human being and noted that her breasts were "remarkably full and well-developed."

Dentists took a special interest in Julia, and several plaster casts were made of her teeth. One set, reportedly of Julia's mouth, is at the Odontological Museum of the Royal College of Surgeons in London. Charles Darwin heard of another set with two rows of teeth in each jaw, "one row being placed within the other."

A British naturalist and writer, Dr. Francis T. Buckland, author of *Curiosities of Natural History,* met Julia and chatted with her. "Her eyes," he wrote, "were deep black, and somewhat prominent, and their lids had long, thick eyelashes; her features were simply hideous on account of the profusion of hair growing on her forehead, and her black beard; but her figure was exceedingly good and graceful, and her tiny foot and well-turned ankle, *bien chaussé* [in a lovely shoe], perfection itself. She had a sweet voice, great taste in music and dancing, and could speak three languages. She was very charitable, and gave largely to local institutions from her earnings. I believe that her true history was that she was simply a deformed Mexican Indian woman."

P. T. Barnum was in London that year, exhibiting Tom Thumb

and giving lectures. Very likely he had seen Julia in the United States; now he wanted to pay her a visit and he got an English showman to introduce him to her. Lent was not present when they arrived and Julia wouldn't take off the heavy veil that hid her face until Lent came in. Barnum, always on the lookout for new oddities, may have offered to exhibit Julia after she returned to the United States. The record tells us nothing about this, however, and Julia was never to leave Europe—not, at any rate, while she was alive.

After London Lent took Julia to other English cities. A warm friendship had grown up between the two. Lent, it was said, taught her to read English and bought books for her. He began to teach her to write. In the long hours of travel, or at night in hotels, reading must have been a wonderful escape for her, a solace in her loneliness. Burying herself in romantic novels, Julia could forget who and what she was; in her imagination she could become a beautiful and adored young woman, like the heroines she read about.

Later in 1857 Lent took Julia to Germany. She performed first in Berlin. He began to think about starring her in a play. Perhaps he had heard of Tom Thumb's success in France acting in a play written especially to exploit his small size. Why couldn't Julia have equal success—in a play that would make the most of her bizarre appearance? Lent found himself a German writer and the piece was quickly put together.

Julia's play opened in Leipzig. It was called *The Farmer Cured.* No copy of it exists, but we can be reasonably certain it featured an actor who played a farmer and Julia, who played—herself. Julia might have been a mysterious woman who always hid her face under a veil, had a lovely voice, and was a wonderful dancer. The farmer might have fallen passionately in love with her and begged her to let him see her face. She, knowing the romance would end the moment she did so, would have kept saying no. When the farmer wasn't onstage the audience could have been treated to comic scenes that exploited Julia's strange features. In the final scene she might reluctantly have given in and lifted the veil—and the farmer would have been cured instantly of his blind passion.

There was a considerable uproar in Leipzig's Kroll Theater the night *The Farmer Cured* opened. The next night it attracted crowds eager to see what the fuss was all about. Among those it attracted were the police. When the curtain fell they let Lent know his play

A portrait of Julia, drawn from life, at the time she was interviewed for the German magazine *Die Gartenlaube*. The artist exaggerated her hairiness.

was offensive and forbade him to put it on again.

The closing of *The Farmer Cured* couldn't have broken Julia's heart. It takes a special toughness to act in front of a rowdy audience, to put up with its rude cries and catcalls, to shrug off its ridicule and insults. Julia went back to her regular program of singing and dancing. The audiences might be smaller—but at least they behaved themselves.

The closing of Julia's play didn't hurt her career. It produced a sensation. One immediate result was that a popular magazine, *Die Gartenlaube,* sent a journalist to interview her and an artist to draw her picture.

Since childhood, the journalist reported, he and the artist had gone to see any human oddity they could. "For sheer monstrosity, however," he wrote, "we can assure you the creature standing before us went far beyond anything we had ever seen." He described Julia's apelike face, her hairiness, her enormous "blood-red" gums, and her teeth. "The position of her teeth is as irregular as their form; the set of teeth in the lower jaw is complete; in the upper jaw only the molars are fully developed." He was struck by her sad look. "In her eyes," he said, "there is a kind of melancholy that arouses sympathy."

When the two Germans entered, the "Mexican Miss," as Lent called her, was working on her toilette. Lent introduced himself as her "guardian" and Julia greeted them with a warm handshake. As the artist drew her portrait the writer asked questions.

The interview was conducted in English and the writer was surprised at the "understanding" and "definiteness" with which Julia expressed herself on every subject that came up. He noted how pleased she sounded as she told him about her triumphant tours in America and England.

The journalist was amused when Julia said she had received more than twenty offers of marriage.

"Why didn't you accept any of them?" he asked.

"They weren't rich enough," Julia replied.

The interviewer strongly suspected Julia's "guardian" had talked this nonsense into "the poor creature." Then he reflected: Perhaps some Yankees actually had wanted to marry her; she might be a monstrosity, but her box-office receipts could make a man rich. If she ever decided to write her memoirs, he concluded, she would have to dictate them, for she was only in the early stages of learning how to write.

At some point in Julia's travels she did receive an offer of marriage. It came from Lent. Some people said he proposed to her because she had earned a great deal of money; he took care of it for her and was afraid she might someday want it back. Other showmen, it was also rumored, were interested in Julia, and Lent, to avoid losing her, decided to ask her to marry him.

Julia said yes. If there were questions about why Lent wanted to take such a strange bride, no one could wonder why she accepted his offer. She was an orphan, with a history of mistreatment, and Lent had been like a father to her. He was her constant companion; he provided the roof over her head, the food she ate, the costumes she wore, the engagements she filled. He encouraged her when her spirits were low, nursed her when she was ill. Any other manager would have done as much. But to poor Julia, unworldly, lonely, and starved for affection, that would have made little difference. She had to love someone, and he was there.

Julia was convinced Lent loved her too. We have her own words for that, preserved by Friederike Gossmann, an actress who knew her. On the morning of Julia's wedding, with a joyful smile making her dark face radiant, she told her friend, "He loves me—he loves me for my own sake."

Friederike Gossmann became a close friend of Julia's and left some interesting impressions of what she was really like. It was quite curious, Gossmann observed, to hear Julia talk about life and the world. These she seemed to know only from her childhood and from books. In show business she hadn't been allowed to have much contact with people; otherwise, her manager thought, the public's curiosity about her would be blunted and she would lose her drawing power.

Still, said Gossmann, when Julia spent time with a person who didn't keep staring at her as a monster—someone who responded to the human being inside, the thinking, feeling creature—she would drop her guard. Forgetting herself, she would reveal a side she usually kept hidden—a side that was childlike and trusting. She would begin to bubble over and laugh and chatter away like any other girl. But, Gossmann added, no matter how lighthearted Julia became, the shadow of sadness never left her eyes.

After Germany, Julia and Lent headed for France. In Paris she found a warm welcome. She and Lent toured the country with a circus, then went on to Russia. Julia was expecting a baby now, but still they kept traveling and exhibiting.

In Moscow, in 1860, Julia gave birth to a son. The baby that was placed in the bed by her side had a head that was covered with hair, long, black, and straight, which ran over his forehead and down the back of his neck. His skin was dark and yellowish. He lived only thirty-six hours.

Julia lay gravely ill. Many Russian aristocrats, we are told, visited her as her condition grew worse. On her deathbed she is reported to have said, "I die happy. I know I have been loved for myself." She was twenty-eight years old.

Although Julia was dead now, her story was far from over.

Julia's body and her son's were taken to the Anatomical Institute of Moscow for an autopsy. Professor Sokolov of the institute took a special interest in them; he regarded them as great curiosities and wanted to preserve them. A businessman to the end, Lent sold the corpses to him for £500, a large sum of money at that time.

What embalming process the professor used isn't known, but the results were extraordinary. When Lent returned to the institute to inspect the bodies he was astonished at how lifelike they looked. Julia and her son might be dead, he decided, but they could still earn money for him. He bought them back for £800. From Sokolov

This startling photograph of Julia Pastrana shows her not alive, as generally believed, but dead. (Compare the pose with that in the next illustration.)

he also obtained a certificate stating these were the authentic bodies of Julia Pastrana and her child, embalmed by him in Moscow.

Lent had a glass display case made, large enough to hold the two bodies. Julia was dressed in one of her colorful embroidered costumes, her coiffure was done, and a necklace and bracelets placed on her. With her eyes (they were glass now) staring sadly and sightlessly before her, she looked much as she had in life. Clothes were made for the child and he was mounted on a stand. The bodies, both rigid because of the remarkable process used to preserve them, were stood up side by side in the glass case.

Lent opened his new exhibit. Julia could not sing or dance anymore, but with her son by her side she seemed to be as great an attraction as ever. Lent traveled with the two corpses throughout Europe. Other showmen quickly recognized the possibilities of the embalmed little family. Obtaining dead bodies (or wax figures), they made them up to look like Julia and her son and exhibited them for years in various countries.*

Two years after Julia's death, in February 1862, Dr. Francis T. Buckland, the naturalist who had met her in London in 1857, received an invitation to examine a great curiosity being shown in that city. He went to the exhibition hall and walked over to "The Embalmed Nondescript," as it was described.

"Julia Pastrana!" he exclaimed.

"Yes, sir," replied the exhibit's owner (it could have been Lent himself), "it *is* Julia Pastrana."

In death Buckland found Julia just as striking as he had in life. "The figure," he wrote, "was dressed in the ordinary exhibition costume used in life, and placed erect upon the table. The limbs were by no means shrunken or contracted, the arms, chest, &c.

---

*Some years ago the author received a letter from an American carnival man who described in convincing detail a very old and battered embalmed body much like Julia's that he had seen in the Soviet Union. The exhibitors told him its name was "Pastrama" and that it had once been accompanied by a baby's body.

retaining their former roundness and well-formed appearance. The face was marvellous; exactly like an exceedingly good portrait in wax, but it was *not* formed of wax. The closest examination convinced me that it was the true skin, prepared in some wonderful way; the huge deformed lips and the squat nose remained exactly as in life; and the beard and luxuriant growth of soft black hair on

An old German poster advertising the exhibition of the embalmed Julia Pastrana and her son. It calls her "The Most Interesting Woman in the World."

and about the face were in no respect changed from their former appearance.

"There was no unpleasantness . . . about the figure; and it was almost difficult to imagine that the mummy was really that of a human being, and not an artificial model."

Buckland didn't mention Julia's baby. Possibly it had been damaged or was no longer fit for display. There is good evidence that it was replaced at least once over the years.

Twenty years later Friederike Gossmann, Julia's friend, saw the two bodies at a fairground in Vienna. A German who wrote under the name of Signor Saltarino also saw them there.

"It was with very peculiar feelings," wrote Saltarino, "that I went up to the glass 'coffin' in which the restless corpse was exhibited. Strange thoughts took hold of me as I looked at the mummy. She stood there in a tawdry gown of red silk, the ghastly grin of the dead on her face. Next to her, in a garment just as tawdry, was her baby, on a perch, like a parrot. Outside the rain was streaming down between the showbooths of Vienna's Prater. The wind raged and whined around the tent. I felt a deep, deep sympathy for the dead woman. She, however, could no longer hear nor see; she felt neither joy nor sorrow, neither lack of love nor my compassion. And I remembered that once she had said with a bright smile, 'He loves me for my own sake.' "*

---

*Lent reportedly married another bearded lady, whom he named Zeñora Pastrana and exhibited along with Julia; he died insane in 1884. The bodies of Julia and her son then passed from one owner to another. Eventually they wound up in Oslo, Norway, where they were exhibited at a carnival. In 1972—more than one hundred years after Julia's death—they were brought to the United States and shown at fairs; they appeared much as Signor Saltarino had described them. Finally withdrawn from exhibition, they were stored away at the carnival in Oslo. In 1979, when the author was in that city, the owner's wife informed him they had recently been stolen.

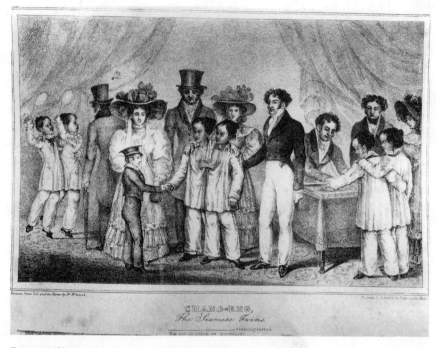

CHANG-ENG,
The Siamese Twins

But yet in truth so matchless

Eng and Chang: three views, in a drawing made during their first visit to England. Note the ligament that binds them together. In pictures, when the twins face forward, Eng is the one on the left.

The
Siamese Twins

Swallows swooped through the tops of the giant bamboo trees that lined both banks of the river. Near the village of Meklong a sampan cut across the water. Inside it Robert Hunter, a Scottish trader, peered in astonishment through the gathering dusk.

He could hardly believe the sight taking place before his eyes.

Not far ahead a bizarre creature was swimming on the surface of the water. It had two heads.

Hunter shut his eyes for a moment. When he opened them the creature was still there. It still had two heads. It also appeared to have eight limbs. They rose and fell rhythmically, in perfect coordination, as the creature sped through the darkening water.

An empty boat bobbed gently dead ahead. The weird animal moved toward it. As the Scot watched, the creature grabbed hold of the side of the boat with four hands and in an instant it had swung itself aboard.

It had been, Hunter suddenly realized, an illusion. It wasn't a single creature. It was actually two—two short, wiry, olive-skinned boys, nude above the waist and each an exact image of the other. In some curious way the two young bodies were joined together physically. Looking hard, he was able to make out the connection.

A short, thick cord of flesh ran from one boy's breast to the other's. Like a chain, it bound them together, close and inseparably.

Hunter gave an order to his boatman and his sampan drew alongside. *"Sawadee,"* he called out, bowing. It was the Siamese greeting.

Placing their hands palm to palm and raising them to their foreheads, the two boys bowed as one. *"Sawadee,"* they replied, their eyes wide with curiosity. Shy but friendly smiles lit their identical oriental faces.

Hunter began to ask them about themselves. The boys, flattered by the interest of the *farang,* answered willingly. By the time the three parted they were fast friends, and Hunter had accepted an invitation to visit them in their home, a houseboat on the river.

In the months that followed, Robert Hunter came to call frequently on Chang and Eng, the extraordinary twin boys he had met that day in 1824. He was always warmly received. Often he brought gifts and, sitting cross-legged on a straw mat, shared meals or drank tea with the little family. Besides the boys it consisted of their widowed mother, Nok, and an older brother and sister. Hunter cultivated their friendship carefully. He asked Nok many questions about the twins, while his eyes tirelessly followed the two bodies that moved about like one. Not only was he very fond of the boys, but in them he felt he had discovered his own fabulous treasure of the East.

The boys, thirteen years old then, had been born on May 11, 1811, on the houseboat. There were many like it in Meklong— houses of bamboo, with roofs of thatched leaves, on rafts, floating on the river.

For their mother, Nok, the birth had been surprisingly easy. The twins had come into the world in a compact little package, the head of one between the legs of the other.

In the Orient a son is valued more highly than a daughter, and Nok was very happy she had given birth to twin boys. But joy turned to confusion when she saw the stout band of tissue that bound them tightly to each other. In the middle of the band there was a single belly button or umbilicus.

In Meklong the conjoined twins were a cause for wonderment; no one there had ever seen or heard of such a birth before. Today we know that Siamese twins are actually not so rare. Physicians estimate that one birth in seventy thousand is of conjoined twins. Most, however, are born dead or die soon after birth.

Conjoined twins are actually a kind of identical twins. Normal identical twins develop from a single egg, which has been fertilized by a single sperm. The egg divides and subdivides, developing into an embryo. Then the embryo splits in two. The twin embryos grow into two completely independent individuals. They share the same sex and, since they have the same genes, the same physical traits.*

Unlike normal identical twins, conjoined twins aren't independent; their bodies are connected. They may be joined back to back, chest to chest, belly to belly, head to head, or in other ways. Sometimes the bodies are incomplete, sharing the same limbs or organs.

Why are some identical twins joined to each other? Biologists offer us two possible explanations. According to one, the original embryo begins to split, but at some point it stops and the twins remain connected. The other possibility: the embryo divides in two completely, but early in their growth the twin embryos collide and grow together—but only in part. Experiments with fish and chick embryos support both explanations.

News of the unusual birth in Meklong spread rapidly. It traveled as far as the capital, Bangkok, sixty miles away, where it reached the ears of the king, Rama II. To the people of old Siam (today's Thailand) an abnormal birth was an evil omen—a sign that heaven was displeased and would punish humankind severely. Rama ordered the twins put to death. But he must have had second thoughts, for his order was never carried out.

The father of the twins was Chinese—a fisherman who had settled in Siam and married a part-Chinese woman, Nok. Because

*Fraternal twins, in contrast to identical twins, develop from two different eggs and sperms. Their genes are not identical.

their parents were Chinese, throughout Siam the twins became known as the Chinese twins. When the rest of the world heard of them, however, they would be called the Siamese twins.*

As newborn infants the twins were held face to face by the short cord of flesh that connected them. But the cord had some give to it, and little by little it stretched. No doubt Nok helped; she had to feed them, wash them, and clothe them, and inevitably these actions pulled on the band. When the babies began to crawl about they stretched it still further.

Nok and her husband named their sons Eng and Chang. In pictures, Eng is the twin on the left, Chang the one on the right. Chang is the shorter of the two.

Like other identical twins the boys looked very much alike, but their personalities were quite different. Chang was more energetic and he had a quicker temper; he also was the smarter of the two and usually the first to make up his mind. Eng was a gentler, shyer, and more easygoing child. Chang was the leader, Eng the follower.

Two people who are so closely linked need to get along well or every day can be a waking nightmare. That was a lesson the boys learned early. When they were young children they got into an argument and began to hit each other hard. Each was in danger of being pounded to a pulp, for even if one had wanted to stop and run away he wouldn't have been able to. Nok heard their grunts and screeches and came running. She pulled them apart—as far as she could pull them apart—and laid down the law to them. They would have to learn to put up with each other, she told them; there was no other way.

The boys understood almost at once. It was something that hardly needed to be put into words for them. They had sensed it

---

*Other conjoined twins had been born before and others have been born since—but because Nok's sons were the first to gain a worldwide reputation all conjoined twins are popularly known as Siamese twins. The term "Siamese" is also applied to certain joined objects—there are, for example, Siamese pipes and Siamese joints.

as babies crawling about on the floor of the houseboat; if they didn't coordinate their movements they simply pulled in different directions and got nowhere. As toddlers they had had to time their little steps together. When they didn't they tumbled to the floor.

Every moment of their lives, waking or sleeping, the boys spent in each other's company. One couldn't go anywhere or do anything unless his brother agreed. If one was cheerful and wanted to play, or was moody and didn't want to play, the other had to go along with his feelings. Each had to love his brother as himself or life would be a misery for both. And so, most of the time, the two lived together on the best of terms.

As the twins grew, the ligament grew with them. It also continued to stretch. When they were twelve it was about five inches long and they were able to stand side by side. The ligament was as thick as a forearm. People were always curious about it and wondered what was inside. When a person touched it exactly in the middle, both Chang and Eng could feel the touch. But if someone touched it closer to one of them, only that boy reacted.

Still the band wasn't especially sensitive. As young children, when somebody lifted one of them up and his brother dangled from the ligament, neither complained that it hurt. The band even had a special advantage. If one twin tripped, the ligament—with his brother standing at the other end of it—often kept him from falling.

Although bound to one another, the twins were able to do almost anything other children did. They could not only run and jump, but dive and swim like porpoises. Their father made them expert fishermen and boatmen at an early age. When he took them out on his sampan they stood at the stern; each held a long pole and guided and propelled the boat with it, after the Siamese fashion.

In 1819, when the boys were eight, a deadly disease hammered Meklong. Cholera took the lives of five of their brothers and sisters; worst of all, it killed their father. Each of the four remaining children and their mother had to work—and work hard—or they would have starved.

Chang and Eng, who had fished for fun before, became fishermen in earnest. After working their nets all day they took their catch to the market—a cluster of boats moored on the river, where merchants sold products of every kind. Shoppers liked to buy from the small boys with their cheerful smiles, their handsome faces, and their remarkable link of flesh. They prospered. They did so well that after a time they gave up fishing, bought merchandise, and sold it in the floating market. They also bred ducks, both to sell and for the eggs, which they preserved with salt, clay, and ashes so they would last a long time.

Meanwhile a new king, Rama III, took his place on the throne of his forefathers. Hearing about the conjoined twins of Meklong, in 1824 he ordered them brought for inspection to his great palace in Bangkok.

For Chang and Eng and their family it was a dizzying honor. Finer garments than any they had ever owned were bought for them. Nok proudly braided their hair in the long pigtails or queues that Chinese people wore. Then the boys, with their mother and sister, were led aboard a big junk by the servants of the king and taken to the capital.

Bangkok, then as now, was a city of a thousand glittering domes and spires. An audience with the king was a solemn affair; the boys were given a thorough course in how to conduct themselves in the presence of awesome Rama. Then they were brought to the king's palace and led into the magnificent audience hall. It was overflowing with soldiers and courtiers. In front, on a high gold-plated throne, under a canopy of gilded umbrellas, sat Rama himself, clad in garments that sparkled with jewels.

Trembling, Chang and Eng got down on their knees as they had been instructed. They raised their folded hands to their foreheads and touched them to the floor nine times. Then they rose and, advancing to the throne, fell to their knees and bowed nine times again.

The king stared down at the two small boys and their strange ligament. They were certainly a curiosity! Speaking through a courtier, he began to fire one question after another at them.

Stammering, the boys replied. Finally, satisfied, Rama gave a royal nod. Gongs clashed through the great hall. Courtiers cried out and fell to their knees. The king disappeared behind a swirl of curtains. Almost frightened out of their wits, the twins flung their arms around each other. Their audience with King Rama had ended.

A circle of elegant courtiers closed in. They studied the amazing ligament, bombarded the boys with questions. Chang and Eng's next stop was the royal harem. King Rama had seven hundred wives and concubines; they and their children were as eager as anybody to inspect the wonders from Meklong. After, the boys were taken to pay their respects to Siam's holy of holies. In the Temple of Gautama they bowed reverently to the Emerald Buddha. It was very, very old and so sacred that no Siamese would ever dare to tell a lie in its presence.

Loaded with gifts, the boys sailed back to Meklong with their mother and sister. Their glory traveled with them. Earlier they had been the village's human oddities; now they were its heroes. Business in the floating market was better than ever.

Not long after the twins' visit to the capital, Robert Hunter, the shrewd Scottish merchant, made an application to the king. By now he was sure he could earn a fortune by exhibiting the boys in the West. But Siam was an absolute monarchy. Every inhabitant was the personal property of the king, and Hunter needed his consent to take the twins abroad. The Scot's request was turned down.

Rama, it seems, also recognized the twins' worth. In 1827 he sent a diplomatic mission to Cochin China (present-day Vietnam). With the mission he sent Chang and Eng. The boys, mounted on an elephant, journeyed from place to place with the Siamese ambassador. They were treated like celebrities and received by the king. Then, with a handsome present from Rama, they were sent home.

For Chang and Eng, life in their native village could never be the same. They had visited exotic, faraway places and been spoken to by great lords. Raising ducks and selling eggs in the floating market seemed terribly humdrum. They longed for an opportunity to travel again.

Two years later that opportunity came. Captain Abel Coffin, master of the American vessel *Sachem,* arrived in Bangkok to trade with the Siamese. An old acquaintance of Robert Hunter's, Coffin was intrigued when the Scot told him of his discovery of the remarkable conjoined twins—and of the piles of money that could be made by exhibiting them in Europe and America. Coffin was even more intrigued when he saw the handsome seventeen-year-olds for himself. He and Hunter promptly formed a partnership to exploit them.

Before the partners could make a move they would need King Rama's consent—which he had refused to Hunter a few years earlier. The boys' mother would also have to give hers.

What about the twins themselves? The partners talked to them. No problem: Chang and Eng could hardly wait to climb aboard Captain Coffin's great white-sailed ship and set out for the other side of the world.

Coffin approached the king. The captain had already won Rama's friendship by selling him hard-to-get firearms. Now Coffin slyly pointed out that the twins, touring the West, would be a living advertisement for the marvels of Rama's wonderful kingdom. His Majesty, flattered, said they could go.

It was Nok who didn't want them to. If Chang and Eng went overseas, she worried, she might never see them again. Coffin and Hunter promised they would be like fathers to the boys; they promised to bring them back safe and sound—and rich—after two and a half years. They offered Nok money too (later they would say it was three thousand dollars). Chang and Eng must also have added their own pleas. Nok finally gave in.

In April 1829, the *Sachem* weighed anchor. The voyage was to take a long time—four and a half months. On shipboard Chang and Eng, with the help of their managers and the friendly American sailors, learned to speak and read some English. They also learned to play checkers—so well, in fact, that they could beat anyone game enough to take them on. With boyish high spirits they would scamper like monkeys up into the ship's rigging, making the hearts of Coffin and Hunter skip more than a few beats.

In August the *Sachem* docked in Boston. Hunter had gone home to Scotland; Captain Coffin had sole charge of the brothers. He quickly hired a business agent, James W. Hale, who was to become a lifelong friend of the twins. Soon the city was papered with signs advertising the exhibition of Chang-Eng, the Siamese Double Boys.

No one in Boston had ever seen living conjoined twins. The city buzzed with rumors that the band connecting Chang and Eng was a fake. To set all doubts at rest, Coffin had the boys examined by a highly respected medical expert, Dr. John Collins Warren, professor of surgery at Harvard. Warren prepared an impressive report certifying they were authentic conjoined twins, and the captain wasted no time in releasing it to the press.

The twins' first shows were very simple. They came out in front of the audience, exhibited the ligament, and answered questions in broken English, with some help from their manager. Three successful weeks later they were off to Providence, Rhode Island, then to New York City. Coffin could see that he and Hunter had made no mistake.

Before long Chang and Eng, prompted by their manager, had begun to develop an act. To the astonishment of the spectators the boys spun head over heels in one rapid somersault after another. Looking around the audience, they would locate an extremely heavy gentleman—sometimes weighing close to three hundred pounds—and carry him a good hundred feet in the hall. For two slender lads just a few inches over five feet tall it seemed unbelievable. They would also play checkers with members of the audience. (They didn't care to play with each other; that, they said, would be like the left hand playing against the right.)

In New York City the twins were again examined. The doctors

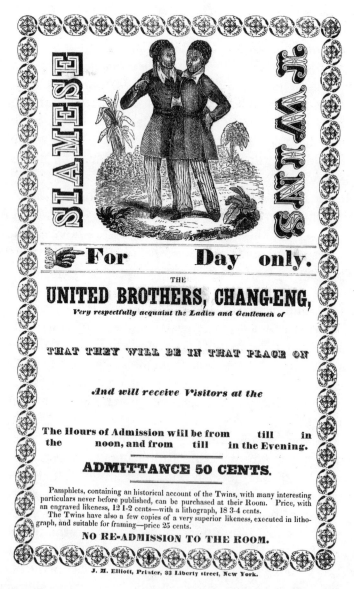

A poster advertising an appearance of the Siamese twins, with blanks still to be filled in. "Chang-Eng" was their professional name and the way they signed their letters.

concluded the ligament had to contain portions of the twins' abdominal organs, such as the intestine, liver, and spleen.* "There can be no doubt," the physicians reported, "that if these boys were separated by the knife, and this band cut across at any part . . . that would expose them to enormous hernial protrusions and inflammations that would certainly prove fatal."

Chang and Eng, after being joined together all their lives, the doctors declared, were "so satisfied with their condition, that nothing renders them so unhappy as the fear of a separation by any surgical operation: the very mention of it causes immediate weeping." Captain Coffin quickly distributed copies of the report to the newspapers.

In October the twins were in Philadelphia. Their exhibition hall was packed day after day. Doctors at Jefferson Medical College showed great interest in them. A leading surgeon, examining the brothers, spoke out against cutting them apart.

Following two good money-making months in the United States Captain Coffin took the twins to England. To protect his and Hunter's investment he had bought ten thousand dollars' worth of insurance on their lives. He had also had stowed in the hold of the ship some unusual items: twelve pounds of mercury and a one-hundred-gallon cask of molasses rum. If the twins were to die during the voyage these supplies could be used to preserve their bodies. Just as the captain had exhibited the living boys he could continue to exhibit their corpses.

For Eng and Chang it was no pleasure trip. While Coffin traveled in first class with his wife and Hale, he skimped on the twins; they traveled steerage. Instead of taking their meals with the passengers, they had to eat with the crew. Coffin described them to the master of the ship as "servants." Later the boys would have other com-

---

*In 1829 a diagnosis like this had to be largely guesswork. The invention of the X-ray machine and other instruments for visualizing the interior of the body lay far in the future.

plaints against the generous Captain Coffin.

In London Hunter was waiting to greet his friends. Mindful of charges in the United States that the twins were a fraud, he invited newspaper editors, political leaders, members of the British nobility, and leading medical men to an advance private showing.

The guests were quickly won over. The same old question came up: Could Chang and Eng be separated without harm to them? Sir Ashley Cooper, Britain's foremost surgeon, replied, "I shouldn't like to try." He saw no point in cutting them apart; they appeared perfectly happy as they were. "Depend on it," he added shrewdly, "those boys will fetch a vast deal more money whilst they are together than when they are separated." Twenty-four physicians signed a document endorsing the exhibition of "these remarkable and interesting youths."

Glowing accounts of the boys appeared in the press. Members of the royal family, including Queen Adelaide, came to see them, as did the Duke of Wellington and many others of the nobility. Everyone was struck by their sweetness, their good manners, their gentle oriental faces. "Their skin," wrote one Englishman, "was soft and smooth, their complexion a dark rich olive, their hair black and shining, and short over the forehead, but left long behind, plaited [in a queue], wound round the head just above the brows, and tied with a long silk tassel which fell over the shoulder."

Chang and Eng looked, it was said, like statues as they stood with their inside arms around each other's shoulders or waists. (These poses were natural since their inside arms were so close together.) Often the twins appeared in Siamese costume. Their English was improving rapidly; they were taking lessons in writing.

Fascinated as they were by the strange new world in which they found themselves, Chang and Eng still missed the old one they had left behind, and especially their mother. "When we saw them on Tuesday," wrote one British reviewer, "though they occasionally smiled, they seemed to move with reluctance, and we discovered nothing of playfulness or merriment in their actions. They evidently longed for a release from their exhibition; for asking the time, and being shown a watch . . . they complained of its being 'too slow.' "

If they were sometimes sad they could also be cheerful, and they often showed a lively sense of humor. Once a Briton tried to convert them from their native Buddhism to Christianity. "Do you know," he asked, "where you would go if you were to die?"

"Yes, yes, up dere," said the boys. They pointed up.

He wanted to drive home the point. "Do you know where I should go if I were to die?"

"Yes, yes," said the boys with a twinkle in their eyes. Their fingers reversed direction. "Down dere."

The twins weren't blind to the charms of the fair sex, nor were the ladies indifferent to theirs. Reportedly, an attractive young woman named Sophia (her surname is not known) fell in love with them. She followed them about, wrote poems to them, and made up her mind to marry them. But she soon discovered that would be impossible. Chang and Eng might be joined together but they were two distinct individuals; to marry them would be bigamy. The boys weren't actually in love with Sophia, but they were flattered by her attention. Naturally press reports of the incident only helped to increase public interest in them.

After seven months in London the boys were taken on a grueling 2,500-mile tour of England, Scotland, and Ireland. In fourteen months they performed before three hundred thousand Britons. Coffin had wanted to exhibit them in France, but the authorities in Paris turned down his application for a visa. Like most people in that age the French believed in the theory of "maternal impressions"—that the unborn child of a pregnant woman might be deformed if some shocking sight or experience frightened her. France wanted to spare its mothers-to-be a bumper crop of Chang-and-Engs.

Robert Hunter, the twins' discoverer, had by now been obliged to return to his business interests in the Orient. He had sold his share in the brothers to Coffin. Leaving for the Far East, he carried with him presents and loving messages from the boys for their mother and other relatives. Coffin had gone back to his ship. With Mrs. Coffin in charge, Chang and Eng sailed back to the United States.

Mrs. Coffin turned out to be as hard and tight-fisted a taskmaster as her husband. Arriving in New York City in March 1831, the twins performed there and were soon en route to Philadelphia and other places. They journeyed from town to town by carriage, often staying just a night or two in each. It was a grinding routine.

After a time the boys, their nerves on edge, showed signs of irritation. Doctors in particular might be annoying; some wanted to make experiments on the brothers. Once, for example, in Massachusetts, a doctor wanted to stick a pin in Chang's shoulder to see if it would have any effect on Eng.

"If you stick a pin in me," said Chang wryly, "my brother Eng might knock you down."

In Alabama their annoyance ended in more than words. A physician came up to the platform and asked to examine the youths' ligament. They didn't enjoy being examined in public and told him so. The physician cried out they were a fake. Chang and Eng, angered, knocked him down. A free-for-all broke out. The brothers were arrested for assault and fined $350.

Later, in Philadelphia, the twins got in trouble again. One patron, shaking Chang's hand, squeezed it so hard it hurt. Chang hit the man and he fell. When he got up he had the brothers arrested for assault and battery.

Chang and Eng were hauled before a magistrate. Chang, the magistrate informed the plaintiff, could be locked up for striking him, but then Eng would have to be locked up too. Jailing Eng, the magistrate continued, would be a clear case of false arrest—and for that the plaintiff himself could face jail. The charge against Chang was quickly dropped.

But the twins had their light moments too. They were fond of playing jokes on people. Once, before they boarded a train, only

Chang bought a ticket. Wrapped in a large cape that hid their connecting band, they climbed aboard and sat down.

The conductor came through, collecting tickets. Chang handed over his. The conductor asked Eng for his ticket.

"I don't have one."

"Then you'll have to buy one or get off the train."

"No, sir, I will *not* buy one. I'll get off the train—but only if my brother does too."

Chang shook his head. "I paid for my ticket and I have every right to stay on board."

The brakeman was called to help put Eng off the train. But when he moved toward the brothers they threw open their cape, revealing the ligament. While he and the conductor stared at it, flabbergasted, the twins burst into laughter and Eng held out the money for another ticket.

May 11, 1832, was Independence Day for Chang and Eng. On that day they turned twenty-one. They were fed up with Captain Coffin and his wife and their pushing, penny-pinching ways. The twins, during their first two years of exhibition, had been paid a scant ten dollars a week. After their return from Europe their wages had finally been raised to fifty dollars, but Mrs. Coffin often begrudged them the money they needed to cover their traveling expenses. The Coffins, the boys felt, had gotten rich exhibiting them, while they themselves had been worked almost mercilessly. Now they declared they were of age and, with Hale as their agent, would shift for themselves. The Coffins were furious but could do nothing to stop them.

Chang and Eng had always felt close to Robert Hunter and kept up a correspondence with him. In one of their letters (written in 1834) they give some insight into their troubles with Coffin.

"He told us," they wrote, "that the arrangement with the Government [of Siam] was for *seven* years, and that 2 1/2 years was mentioned to our mother in order to quiet her fears and prevent any obstacle from being in the way of our leaving home with him.

The Siamese twins in 1839. The booklet displayed was sold at their exhibitions.

However, this kind of double dealing was but badly calculated to induce us to remain with him any longer. . . . We have nearly completed the tour of the United States, being now in the 19th state of the 24 which compose the Union."

They also spoke of their desire to return to Siam. This was a wish they expressed time and time again. Once, when an American woman told them she was going to Siam and intended to visit their mother, they gave her a message for their family.

"Tell them we are coming home sometime," said Chang. And Eng added: "When we have money enough."

But, despite their best intentions, they were never to see their homeland again.

With Charles Harris, a new manager, they now began to tour on their own. Their business ledgers, which have come down to us, provide a picture of their activities. The expense items include a buggy they bought and a horse named Bob. "Opeldoc," a horse liniment, cost them twenty-five cents; so did having their jackets mended. One interesting item was 18 3/4 cents for "Catching the horse Bob." Another was "Hire of an ox team to draw us out of mud 25¢." When they visited Kenyon College in Ohio they listed an expense of four dollars for a biography of a favorite poet of theirs, Lord Byron, which they presented to the college.

For years the twins traveled around the country tirelessly, giving their show in hundreds of towns and cities. Their agents usually went before them to place advertisements, put up posters, and hire halls. The admission charge was fifty cents. The brothers also sold pamphlets telling their story, pictures of themselves, and sometimes cigars.

In 1836, with their manager, Chang and Eng returned to Europe. This time they toured France (which now raised no objection), Belgium, and Holland. They enjoyed making new friends and seeing sights they had read about in books. Then it was back to the United States and the same old wearing routine of travel and exhibition in familiar places.

For Chang and Eng the life of wandering showmen was losing its luster. They itched to settle down somewhere. In 1839, ten years after they first arrived in the United States, they finally did. The place they chose was the town of Wilkesboro, in the foothills of the Blue Ridge Mountains of North Carolina. They were keen hunters and fishermen, and the state's woodlands and streams teemed with game. They had saved a tidy sum, more than ten thousand dollars. It wasn't enough to retire on, of course; they would have to do something to earn a living. Merchants they had been in their boyhood in Siam, and merchants they would be again. And so they stocked and opened a country store.

The store was a failure, so later that year they gave it up and bought a hundred and fifty acres at Trap Hill. There they built a four-room house and set themselves up as farmers.

Now that Chang and Eng had a home, they were ready to strike, permanent roots in America. That same year they raised their right hands in the Superior Court and took the oath of allegiance to the United States. Court documents show they still had only first names, the custom in Siam. As Americans they would need a surname. They had good friends in New York City named Bunker (Chang had even been in love with a daughter of the family) and now they went to court and adopted that name. Henceforth they would be Chang and Eng Bunker.

In a letter to Robert Hunter the twins tell him their situation in 1842. "We have bought some land in this country, and raise our own corn and hogs—we enjoy ourselves pretty well, but have not as yet got married. But we are making love pretty fast, and if we get a couple of nice wives we will be sure to let you know about it. We weigh 220 lbs. (together) and are pretty stout fellows at that!!!!"

They were "making love pretty fast. . . ."

Near Wilkesboro lived David Yates, a well-to-do farmer who had six children. Chang and Eng had met two of his young daughters, Adelaide and Sallie, and taken a fancy to them. They often called at Farmer Yates's home. As celebrities and men who had seen more of the world than most, they were very welcome guests. Sometimes they serenaded the two young ladies with their flutes.

In the next few years a warm affection developed between the twins and the sisters. It grew warmer and deeper. The first time the two couples appeared in public the good people of Wilkesboro were shocked—but not so much as Mr. and Mrs. Yates when their daughters told them they were in love with Chang and Eng and wanted to marry them. The girls were ordered never to see the twins again; Chang and Eng were forbidden to call. For the brothers it was a painful blow. It was also a bitter reminder of something they had begun to forget—how different they were from other human beings.

The girls pleaded and wept, but their parents refused to change their minds. Adelaide, nineteen, and Sallie, twenty, were independent and strong-willed. Nothing, they resolved, would stop them from marrying the men they loved. The two couples met in secret and arranged to elope. But before they could carry out their plan the parents gave in. On April 13, 1843, a double wedding was celebrated at the Yates farm. "May the connection be as happy as it will be close!" wished a local newspaper.

Chang and Eng and their brides moved into the four-room house at Trap Hill. Within a year both twins were fathers, and babies kept arriving regularly after that. The birth of each child was entered in a ledger Chang and Eng kept. They recorded no more than the date and the name of each child; they never felt any need to show who the parents were. By the time, many years later, that the last name was entered, they had twenty-one children between them. Eleven were Eng's, ten Chang's.*

The twins continued to buy land and did well as farmers. They

*Very few Siamese twins marry, and fewer still have children. Chang and Eng, with their twenty-one, hold the world's record. Their children had children, and recently there were about one thousand living descendants, including a United States Air Force general and a railroad president. Many still make their home in North Carolina.

The twins and their wives with their brood of eleven children.

moved to a larger house near the village of Mount Airy. Later, when even that became too small for the growing families and the twins began to have disagreements (so, it is said, did their wives), they bought a second house nearby and Chang's wife and children moved into it.

Although the families had divided up, the twins could not. Henceforth they split their time between the two houses, spending three days in one, then three days in the other. Neither bad weather nor ill health, nor even, once, the tragic death of a child, was ever allowed to interfere with this schedule. Each brother, they also agreed, was to be the master of both in his own home. When the twins were in Chang's house, Chang would be in command and Eng would have to go along with what his brother wanted. In Eng's house Eng would be the master.

At first the twins shared their land as partners; after the families split up the brothers divided their property and each ran his own farm. Keen students of scientific agriculture, they used the most up-to-date farming equipment and methods. Tobacco, wheat, potatoes, oats, and corn were some of the crops they grew; their livestock included pigs, sheep, fowl, cattle, and milk cows. Like other Southerners of the time, they owned slaves.

Chang and Eng were well known and well liked in their community. They helped to build the local Baptist church and they attended it. They took pleasure in entertaining their neighbors. Eng was devoted to playing cards and checkers, but Chang found the games dull; when the brothers were in Eng's house, where Chang's wishes came second, he often dozed or read while his brother played with his friends or children.

Although the twins had had no schooling in the United States, they loved books. They were especially fond of history and poetry and often read aloud to each other or to their families. Because of their extensive reading and travels they were widely respected as educated men.

Crack shots with both rifle and pistol, Chang and Eng enjoyed taking part in shooting matches. They loved to hunt, too, and frequently went out after possum with their slaves. Wolves sometimes plagued the local farmers' domestic animals. The brothers' skill as marksmen became a legend when, hearing noises from their livestock one night, they rushed out and killed a wolf notorious for preying on their neighbors' animals.

One of their special pleasures was chopping down trees and helping their neighbors build their homes. According to an old tradition, the brothers developed their own timesaving method of felling trees, which became known as the double chop. Taking up a position next to a tree, Chang would hit the trunk with his axe at an angle; his brother would then strike at the opposite angle. Bound to each other as they were, it was the most natural and quickest way to work.

As the names of more and more little Bunkers were set down

The ligament binding the twins together did not stop them from hunting, fishing, farming, or doing most of the other things more normal people do, as this Currier and Ives print illustrates.

in the ledger, the brothers foresaw their farm profits would not pay for the good educations they wanted for their children. In 1849 they decided to go back on the show circuit. In 1853 they made another tour, and another in 1860; both times each twin brought along one of his children to take part in the show. In 1860, when they were forty-nine, they were featured attractions at P. T. Barnum's celebrated American Museum in New York City. Their relationship with the master showman wasn't always smooth. They thought he was too tight with money and they let him know it.

Mark Twain, creator of Tom Sawyer and Huckleberry Finn, took a special interest in twins and in human oddities. Chang and Eng, who were examples of both, inevitably became a subject for his pen. In 1868 he wrote a humorous essay, "The Siamese Twins," in which he pretended to be closely acquainted with them. One of the twins, he said, tongue in cheek, had been born two years before his brother. "By an understanding between themselves," he wrote, "Chang does all the indoor work and Eng runs all the errands. . . ." Later, during the Civil War, according to Twain, both fought gallantly, "Eng on the Union side and Chang on the Confederate. They took each other prisoners at Seven Oaks. . . ."

Surprisingly enough, Twain's account was almost partly true. The name of one of the twins actually came up in a draft for the Union Army.

When the first shots of the war rang out at Fort Sumter in 1861, Chang and Eng sided staunchly with the South. Two of their sons bore arms in the Confederate Army. In 1865, as the war was drawing to a close, the Union Army swept into North Carolina, and Mount Airy was occupied by Federal troops. The commanding general ordered some local residents drafted into his forces. The names of all males—including those of Eng and Chang Bunker—were placed in a lottery. Eng's name was one of those drawn. When the Union officers realized who he was, they immediately dropped all claim to him.

The Civil War left the South in ruins, and with it the fortunes of the twins. Earlier they had lent out large sums of money at interest. As the war went on, the value of the Confederate dollar fell almost to zero. It was with these dollars that the twins' debtors repaid them. Also, the brothers, between them, had owned thirty-three slaves, their most valuable asset. At war's end not only were the slaves free; for the first time the brothers had to pay them for their labor.

Unable to make ends meet, Chang and Eng had to go back into show business. They were middle-aged men now—not the handsome, athletic youths they once had been—and over the years so many Americans had seen them that they couldn't attract the public the way they once had. Business was bad until someone suggested their wives should appear with them. The public was very curious

A publicity photograph of the twins, taken in 1865 by Mathew Brady, Abraham Lincoln's favorite photographer. In front of Eng and his wife, Sallie *(left)*, sits their son Patrick. Chang's son Andrew sits in front of his father and his mother, Adelaide.

to get a good look at the women who had married the Siamese twins and box-office receipts picked up.

In New York City Chang and Eng signed up with P. T. Barnum once more. The showman worked out a special tour for them, this time with two of their daughters. "I sent them to Great Britain," he wrote in his autobiography, "where, in all the principal places, and for about a year, their levees [exhibitions] were continually crowded. In all probability the great success was enhanced, if not actually caused, by extensive announcements in advance that the main purpose of Chang-Eng's visit to Europe was to consult the most eminent medical and surgical talent with regard to the safety of separating the twins."

The main purpose of the trip was, of course, to make money. But separation from one another was actually very much on the twins' minds. Their wives, Sallie and Adelaide, wanted to have their husbands to themselves all the time, without a brother-in-law as a constant companion. With the years, too, the twins had been disagreeing more and more. One important reason was that Chang had become an alcoholic. His drunkenness was a heavy burden to Eng, who didn't drink, and it led to violent arguments. If they could only be separated, the brothers believed, most of their problems would disappear. And so, during their tour, they called on some of Britain's major surgeons. As in the past, the surgeons declared that separating the twins would be extremely dangerous.

The following year Chang and Eng returned to Europe, this time touring Germany and Russia. Again they consulted doctors about a separation; again the answer was no.

On the voyage home Chang suffered a stroke. His right side was paralyzed. From that time on he had to hobble about on a crutch, his right foot supported by a strap held by his brother. Always the more difficult of the pair, Chang became more irritable than ever. He drank even more heavily.

Mark Twain, in his sketch about the twins, described Eng as a drunk and Chang as an enemy of drink—just the opposite of the true situation. When Eng got intoxicated, Twain wrote, the liquor traveled through the ligament connecting the twins and Chang found he was getting drunk in spite of himself.

The reality was different. Chang's drinking had no physiological effect on Eng. But it did make his life harder. Chang, at home, was free to drink himself senseless if he had a mind to. Eng, chained at his side, could not move until his brother sobered up.

They clashed more and more. After one particularly savage argument Eng pulled his twin into his buggy and drove him to their physician, Dr. Joseph Hollingsworth. They told the doctor life together was unbearable and demanded an immediate separation. Hollingsworth agreed to perform the operation but he made one thing clear: the surgery would kill them both. Their tempers cooled down and they made peace with each other.

Chang's stroke brought other changes. No longer could the twins work on their farms, something they had always enjoyed. No longer could they hunt or travel or exhibit. Life was narrowing down. Sooner or later—and most likely sooner—one of them would die. They arranged with their doctor that when that happened he would come at once and sever the cord so the living twin might have a chance to go on living.

In January 1874, while the brothers were at Chang's house, he had a bad attack of bronchitis and the doctor was called. After two days Chang felt a little better. The time had come for the move to Eng's place but the weather was cold and raw. Both Eng and Adelaide, Chang's wife, urged him to stay where he was. He would have none of that. So the twins climbed into an open buggy and drove to Eng's place.

The next day Chang felt worse. That night, when the two were in bed, he woke his brother and complained he was finding it hard to breathe. They got out of bed—they slept in a bedroom downstairs—and went out on the porch. Chang took long, deep breaths of the cold night air. Then they went back to bed.

Later Eng felt someone shaking him. It was Chang. He said he felt terribly cold; he wanted to get up and light a fire in the fireplace.

"I don't want to get up," said Eng. "It's warmer in bed."

Grumbling, Chang gave in.

Before long Chang shook his twin awake once more. His voice was trembling. "It's hard for me to breathe, lying in bed like this, Eng."

The two got up, put fresh logs in the fireplace, and lit them. For an hour they sat together close to the warming blaze. Eng, very tired, finally persuaded Chang to come back to bed.

Upstairs, Eng's wife, Sallie, and his children were sleeping. Dur-

Eng and Chang in 1870. That year Chang suffered a stroke that left him paralyzed on one side.

ing the night some of the children heard one of the twins call out. Then the calling stopped and the children went back to sleep.

At 4:00 A.M. Eng's son William came downstairs and opened the twins' bedroom door. He looked at his father. Eng was deep in sleep. Going to the other side of the bed, William peered at Chang by the light of the lamp.

Chang was terribly still.

William looked down closer. A chill ran through him. His uncle was dead.

Eng stirred. "I feel mighty sick," he told his son. "How is your uncle Chang?"

"Uncle Chang is dead."

Shocked, Eng turned to look at his brother. Violent nervous spasms shook him. "Then I am going too!" he gasped.

William raced upstairs and awakened the family. They all rushed down to the bedroom, and Sallie hustled one of the boys off to call the doctor. The time to separate the brothers had come.

Eng was drenched with sweat. "I am very bad off," he moaned. Terrible cramps wracked his limbs. He begged Sallie and the children to massage his arms and legs. They worked over him in frantic haste and tried to comfort him.

"I am choking," groaned Eng. He tugged at Chang's body, pulling it closer, as if that would help him to breathe.

The doctor, they told him, would soon be there and he would be all right.

Eng seemed to calm down. His voice sounded very weak. "May the Lord have mercy on my soul," they heard him whisper. He closed his eyes and slept.

The snow was deep and the doctor lived miles away. When he arrived Eng could not be awakened.

The deaths of Chang and Eng Bunker, the original Siamese twins, aroused interest around the world. Their bodies were removed to Jefferson Medical College in Philadelphia, where an autopsy was performed. Inside the ligament were found portions of their liver tissue and an artery that connected their circulatory systems. Could either (or both) of the twins have survived a separation by surgery? Given the medical procedures available in their time, it seems doubtful. With modern surgical techniques, however, Siamese twins can be separated, but only if their connections are not too complex.

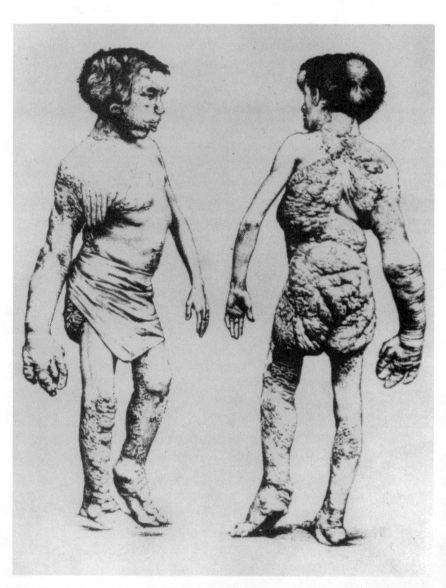

Two views of Joseph Merrick in 1884, when he was first examined by Treves. His disorder was later identified as neurofibromatosis.

The
Elephant Man

T he year was 1884, the month was November, and the day was chilly and bright. When Frederick Treves arrived the shop was closed, but he knew at once he had found the place he was looking for.

Spread across the front window Treves saw an enormous canvas poster painted in screaming bright colors. Against a background of palm trees stood a huge figure—a figure so weird he would not forget it as long as he lived.

What made the figure unforgettable was that it was not completely human. Part of it was a man, all right—but part of it was a beast.

It was a creature out of a nightmare. Mounted on human shoulders was the great gray domed head of an elephant. The body, except for a loincloth wrapped around its middle, was naked. It seemed normal enough until you looked at the right arm and the legs below the knee. These were monstrously big—and they were covered not with human skin but with the wrinkled gray hide of an elephant.

"SEE THE ELEPHANT MAN!" the poster commanded. "INCREDIBLE! SHOCKING! ADMISSION TWOPENCE."

Across the road from where Treves stood in London's busy East End loomed an imposing long red-brick structure. It covered acres and acres. It was in fact the largest hospital not just in Great Britain but in the whole world. Frederick Treves, only thirty-one years old, was an up-and-coming surgeon on the staff of the London Hospital. He was also a brilliant anatomist and lectured at the hospital's medical college. When he had learned that in a shop across from the hospital a showman was exhibiting an extraordinary human curiosity called the Elephant Man, he hurried over to see it.

The showman finally appeared and unbolted the door. The shop was empty, cold, and dusty, and cutting off the back of it was a red curtain hanging from a cord. Treves could see he was to be an audience of one. After collecting a shilling from him, the showman tugged the curtain aside.

In the semidarkness, crouching on a stool, sat a bent, eerie-looking figure huddled under a brown blanket. It was illuminated only by the faint blue flame of a gas jet over which the figure leaned, trying to keep warm.

"Stand up!" cried the showman.

The thing slowly climbed to its feet and the blanket fell from its shoulders.

Almost every day in the week Treves coolly and calmly examined or operated on patients who were terribly deformed or maimed by disease or injury. Now, however, he was shocked to find himself instinctively drawing back.

In nine years of medical practice never had he beheld a human being so horrible looking.

The Elephant Man, naked to the waist, shivered in the cold. His feet were bare and his only garment was an old pair of black trousers. A little more than five feet tall, he appeared even shorter because his back was bowed. His head, huge and unevenly shaped, seemed almost as large around as his waist. Great bony masses projected all over it; one, larger than a tangerine, almost covered one eye. The right side of the cranium bulged outward behind his ear. From the back of his head hung a bag of purplish, spongy, cauliflowerlike flesh; another grew down in front of his right shoulder. A deformity of the upper jaw had so twisted his nose and upper lip that they resembled an elephant's tusk or trunk.

The creature's back was just as unsightly. Covering it almost entirely—and hanging down like curtains as far as midthigh—were heavy baglike masses of spongy flesh. The skin was warty and purplish.

Masses of the same ugly flesh hung from the Elephant Man's right arm, which was abnormally large and deformed. The enormous hand—it was more like a paddle or a fin—seemed almost useless. His other arm, curiously, was completely normal but no larger than that of a girl ten years of age, and ended in a beautiful hand.

The little man's lower legs were swollen and misshapen almost as badly as his right arm. One foot was almost clubbed. Disease of the hip had left him permanently lame; he leaned on a cane as he stepped in front of Treves. From the funguslike bags of flesh that hung from his body rose a sickening odor.

A wave of pity swept over the surgeon. Then scientific curiosity crowded in; he felt he needed to study the unfortunate fellow more closely, to learn more about him.

Treves asked the little man questions. The creature mumbled something, but the surgeon couldn't understand a word.

The exhibitor helped out. The Elephant Man's name was Merrick,* he said. He was in his early twenties and he was from Leicester.

Treves gave the showman some money and arranged to have Merrick come to his office in the medical college. But this immediately raised a question in his mind: How could the Elephant Man

---

The Elephant Man's first name was Joseph. Treves, however, in writing about him, referred to him as "John Merrick"; this mistake has been perpetuated in the play The Elephant Man, *by Bernard Pomerance, and in the motion picture of the same title.*

get across the street without gathering a crowd and being taken in custody by the police?

The answer, the exhibitor showed him, was simple. When the Elephant Man went out he wore a hat and a cloak that completely concealed him. The hat, shaped like a yachting cap, had all around it a flannel cloth that hung down over his head; a wide horizontal slit in front allowed him to see. The long billowing black cloak hid his ungainly body. To complete the costume he had a pair of baglike slippers to cover his deformed feet.

Even so, it seemed best for him to go over in a cab. In Merrick's hand the surgeon placed his calling card. He told him to show it to the porter when he arrived; it would ensure his admittance to the college.

The following day, hidden from view by his cloak and cap, and leaning heavily on his cane, Merrick limped into Treves's office. The

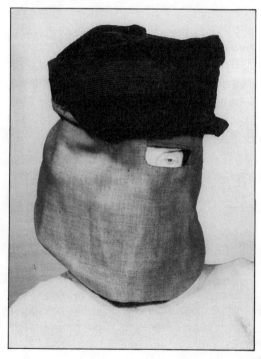

The cap and mask worn by Joseph Merrick, the Elephant Man.

surgeon asked him to take off his clothes. In the bright light of day the little man's condition appeared even more frightful than in the semidarkness of the shop.

Treves had a photographer take pictures of him. Then he asked Merrick many questions. The enlarged, distorted bones of his jaw made it impossible for him to speak clearly. But Treves gathered he was the only one in his family who had his strange disorder. He had been deformed since childhood; with the years his condition had grown steadily worse.

The cause of his trouble, Merrick told the surgeon, was an accident that had happened to his mother while she was pregnant with him. A circus had come to Leicester and paraded its animals through the city. Standing in the pushing crowd of onlookers, Mrs. Merrick had been thrust out into the street. She had fallen directly in the path of a huge elephant.

The poor woman was dazed and bewildered. She saw the beast's foot was about to come smashing down upon her. Pulling herself together, she managed to roll out of the way just in time. But the fright and shock of the experience had left their mark, or so the unhappy woman always believed. Her son had developed a big head like an elephant's and enormous legs covered with skin like an elephant's.

All through the visit the little man appeared confused and afraid. The twisted words he slobbered from his gash of a mouth were hard to understand. Poor fellow, thought Treves, he must be retarded. Lucky for him! How terrible it would be if he really knew how dreadful his condition is!

Of the Elephant Man's disease the young anatomist could make nothing. Never had he seen or read of anything like it. But he was determined to do everything he could to learn more about it and help its victim.

Would Merrick be willing to come to a meeting of the Pathological Society, he asked. Some of the greatest surgeons and physicians in Britain would be present. One or two of them might be able to cast some light on his mysterious disorder.

The little man paused. Any hope he had of a cure had turned to ashes long ago. But now, warmed by the surgeon's sympathy and interest, the ashes began to glow again. He nodded.

The meeting of the Pathological Society was a disappointment. No one there had ever run into a disorder anything like Merrick's. Saddened, the Elephant Man slunk back to his lonely life in the sideshow. But Treves was no quitter; he couldn't stop puzzling over the case.

He soon went back to the shop across from the hospital. The door was locked, the poster gone from the window. The police, he found out, had shut down the exhibition; they considered it too brutal and degrading for the public to see. No one could tell him where the showman and the Elephant Man had taken themselves off to.

Two years passed. One day, at the hospital, a police constable called and asked for Treves. He reported that a severely deformed person dressed in a long black cloak and a huge hat with a mask had turned up at the Liverpool Street railroad station. A crowd had been mocking and baiting him until the police came to his rescue.

The officers couldn't make out a word the deformed man said. Finally he fished something out of his pocket. The constable placed it in the surgeon's hand. It was a small piece of cardboard, and printed on it was the name of Frederick Treves, lecturer in anatomy at the London Hospital Medical College.

In the railroad station waiting room the constable led the surgeon to what looked like a bundle of rags piled in a corner. The bundle stirred. Treves bent over and found himself staring into the pathetic twisted face of Joseph Merrick. The little man was so exhausted and hungry he couldn't say a word. But he made a sound as if he was pleased to see the surgeon.

There was only one place to take him. Treves helped him to his feet and in a few minutes they were in a hansom cab, rattling over the cobblestones on the way to the London Hospital.

Where in the hospital, Treves wondered, could poor Merrick be made comfortable? Certainly not in a crowded ward, where all day long he would have to face the stares and mutterings—curious or cruel—of other patients. The surgeon finally found a place; high up in the attic there were tiny rooms where serious cases were isolated, and in one of these Merrick was bedded down.

Sir Frederick Treves, distinguished surgeon and anatomist and the physician who took care of the Elephant Man. (Portrait by Sir Luke Fildes.)

The first disaster was quick in coming. A young wardmaid fetched food for the Elephant Man from the kitchen. Nobody had thought to prepare her for what she would see when she pushed open his door. The instant she laid eyes on the misshapen head and face she screamed; the tray crashed to the floor and she ran from the room. For the unfortunate man lying on the bed it was not a new experience.

The second disaster—one much more serious—lay just ahead. In admitting his patient, Treves had broken an unbreakable rule. The London Hospital was a general hospital. It accepted only cases in need of active treatment. Chronic cases—and Merrick's was a chronic case—had to go elsewhere. He could stay only until he recovered from his exhaustion.

Examining the little man, Treves found he was much worse than he had been two years earlier.

I can't send someone in Merrick's condition out into the streets, the surgeon said to himself. That would be too cruel. The chairman of the hospital, Treves knew, was a sensitive, kindly man. If anyone could help, he could. The surgeon headed for the office of F. C. Carr Gomm.

The pathetic sight of the Elephant Man and his sad story brought tears to the chairman's eyes. "Mr. Carr Gomm," Treves wrote afterward, "not only was good enough to approve my action but . . . agreed with me that Merrick must not again be turned out into the world."

That didn't mean the Elephant Man could stay in the London Hospital indefinitely, however. He would have to go somewhere else. But Britain had hospitals for the incurable; Carr Gomm promised he would do everything in his power to get one of them to take the little man in.

In the days that followed, the surgeon visited Merrick often. "I very soon learned his speech so that I could talk freely with him," Treves wrote. Merrick, he discovered, far from being retarded, was actually "remarkably intelligent." He loved to read. He was fond of poetry. "The delight of his life was a romance, especially a love romance." Of the real world he seemed to know very little. He had a deep fear of people, as they had shunned him or abused him since he was a child.

Joseph Carey Merrick had been born on August 5, 1862, the son of a warehouseman. At birth he looked like any other baby; but before long curious changes appeared in him. Inside his mouth a hard tumor started to grow and grow, until it pushed out like a tusk. Both of his lower legs began to enlarge abnormally; so did his right arm, and his skin became loose and rough. On his forehead a lump of bone formed. Then another formed, and another, until his head was oversized and misshapen.

To the boy's unhappy mother these disturbing signs meant only one thing: her experience of almost being crushed beneath the elephant's foot had marked her poor son forever.

No one in those days understood what was the matter with Joseph. It was 1909 (long after his death) before scientists succeeded in diagnosing his condition. Today, because of him, it is sometimes called "elephant man's disease." Neurofibromatosis (abbreviated NF) is its scientific name; it is also called von Recklinghausen's neurofibromatosis for the German doctor who first described it.

In NF, tumors form on the nerves. These tumors may appear inside the bones, on the skin, beneath it, inside the organs, or anywhere else, since nerves are present all through the body. Half of all cases of NF arise spontaneously, by genetic mutation, the other half by inheritance.

NF is one of the commonest nerve disorders. It affects all races and both sexes equally. In the United States today about one hundred thousand people have it. In Britain there are twenty thousand cases; throughout the world perhaps a million. Many are quite mild. In most the only symptoms may be a half-dozen or more large brown spots on the skin and a few tumors; some people with NF aren't even aware they have it. Frequently the symptoms can be concealed under clothing, and often the disorder doesn't interfere with a person's ability to work, lead a normal life, and marry. Having children is another matter. A child stands a fifty percent chance of inheriting the disorder when one parent has it.

If an NF patient develops tumors, usually they are benign; in only a small percentage of cases do they turn cancerous. Other complications may include mental retardation, blindness, deafness, paralysis, epilepsy, or a spine condition called scoliosis, which Joseph had.

Very likely Joseph's case, overall, is the most severe one on record.

Nowadays NF is fairly well understood, but even a hundred years after Joseph's death no cure is known. However, if the disorder can't be cured it can be helped. Doctors can provide relief for many of the symptoms by surgery or other means. As with Joseph, the emotional problems may be very serious; in many cases psychiatric treatment proves valuable. Although researchers haven't found the faulty genes that cause the different kinds of NF, in historic breakthroughs in 1987 they determined the chromosomes where two of the genes are located—a promising sign that effective treatment and a cure may be possible before long.*

Joseph's increasing deformities never stopped his mother from loving him. The greatest misfortune of his life came, he thought, when he was ten: his mother died of pneumonia. "Peace to her," he wrote years later in a brief autobiography, "she was a good mother to me." His most treasured possession was a picture of her. Looking at it, he used to wonder how so beautiful a woman could have had such a monster as himself for a child.

Before long his father took another wife. "Henceforth," Joseph

---

*The National Neurofibromatosis Foundation, 141 Fifth Avenue, New York, N.Y. 10010, supports research into the disorder and provides information and guidance for those who need it.

wrote, "I never had one moment's comfort." His stepmother had completely normal children of her own, and she had no patience with her husband's disfigured son.

When the boy was twelve he had to leave school. The new Mrs. Merrick made his life "a perfect misery," he would recall; "lame and deformed as I was, I ran, or rather walked away from home two or three times, but suppose father had some spark of parental feeling left, so he induced me to return home again." During these brief escapes from the unpleasantness at home he took refuge with an uncle.

"When about thirteen years old," Joseph wrote, "nothing would satisfy my stepmother until she got me out to work; I obtained employment at Messrs Freeman's, Cigar Manufacturers, and worked there about two years, but my right hand got too heavy for making cigars, so I had to leave them."

The second Mrs. Merrick couldn't stand having the handicapped boy around the house. She insisted he go out and find a new job.

Nobody would hire a boy in his condition. After hours of dragging himself from factory to factory in vain, he would get hungry and come home for a bite. His stepmother pounced on him at once, screaming he didn't want to find work. "I was taunted and sneered at so that I could not go home to my meals, and used to stay in the streets with an hungry belly rather than return for anything to eat; what few half-meals I did have, I was taunted with the remark— 'That's more than you have earned.' "

His father next got him a peddler's license. Filling a tray with gloves, stockings, and other items, he hung it around the boy's neck and sent him out to sell from door to door. Each day he was expected to sell a definite amount of goods. This he found harder and harder as the tusk sticking out of his mouth made him more unsightly and his speech more difficult to understand. "Being deformed, people would not come to the door to buy my wares."

One day the boy, who never had enough to eat, spent his

earnings for food. Later he headed for home, dreading the welcome he was sure to receive.

It turned out worse than he expected. His father gave him a terrible beating. Home was no longer home. He didn't have to think about what to do: he had to run away. His nights he spent in cheap lodging houses, his days trudging through the streets, selling what he could and eating as little as possible.

His father didn't come looking for him, but his kindly uncle did. When he found Joseph he insisted the boy come to live with him and his family. In his uncle's home, life was good for Joseph—as good as it could be for someone with his handicaps who had to earn his living peddling. But after two years . . .

"My deformity had grown," he wrote. "I could not move about the town without having a crowd of people gather round me." Because of his bizarre appearance the city refused to renew his peddler's license. Suddenly he was unable to earn a penny toward his support. Nor could his aunt and uncle afford to keep him any longer; they were hard up themselves and they were expecting another child. There was only one place he could turn to.

The English workhouse was the refuge of last resort for paupers. It took care, at the expense of the community, not only of the unemployed but of those who were too sick, too old, or too young to take care of themselves. Any who were physically able were obliged to work. For the impoverished of its time the workhouse did what the welfare system does today.

To poor Joseph life in Leicester Workhouse seemed even grimmer than it had in his stepmother's house.

The long workday began at five: bells clanged to turn him and the other inmates out of their hard beds. After a breakfast of bread and gruel they began their tasks. Some chopped wood, broke up old hemp, pounded stone into chips; others did the laundry, scrubbed the floors, or worked in the vegetable garden. Rules were strict and anyone who broke them faced severe punishment. Joseph felt like a prisoner and, dressed in a coarse uniform, he even looked like one. He was surrounded by wretched, unhappy people—many were misfits or drunkards who insulted or tormented him.

The boy's physical condition never stopped going downhill. The monstrous tumor in his upper jaw in particular made him miserable. Close to nine inches long by now, it turned his upper lip inside out; when he ate, much of the food fell out of his mouth.

One day a doctor, examining the inmates, took notice of the growth in Joseph's mouth and ordered him to the infirmary. On the operating table a scalpel cut away three or four ounces of tumor. Then he was sent back to the workhouse treadmill.

Joseph's life of drudgery and despair was becoming more than he could stand. He longed to escape from the workhouse—but where could he go? Nothing short of a miracle, he knew, could help him.

After four and a half years he made that miracle happen.

There lived in Leicester a showman who was interested in exhibiting unusual performers, including human curiosities. With his strange deformities, thought Joseph, he might just qualify. A letter to the showman brought him promptly to the workhouse. He looked Joseph over and, to his astonishment, gave him a warm, approving smile. On August 3, 1884, hardly daring to believe his good luck, Joseph limped away from the workhouse. He was free at last!

A completely different, exciting life opened up for the twenty-two year old. First he was given a professional name: The Elephant Man. Then he was launched on a tour that took him from town to town, from music hall to carnival to country fair. His exhibitors gave him half of what his show brought in and provided him with shelter, clothing, and protection. He received from them, he said, "the greatest kindness and attention." He was self-supporting—on his own for the first time in years.

This happy period was to last a year and a half. Joseph had been on the show circuit only four months when he attracted the attention of Frederick Treves. But he also attracted the attention of the police, and as time went by they objected more and more to his exhibition. Finally his managers turned him over to an Austrian showman, who talked of better opportunities on the Continent. But even there the police wouldn't leave him in peace.

The end came in Brussels. One day Joseph found the Austrian had disappeared—and so had Joseph's hard-earned savings of £50, a large sum in those times. Abandoned, penniless, without a friend, in a foreign land, he had to sell almost everything but the clothes on his back to raise the fare back to England.

At every step of the journey home the handicapped youth was met with insult and ill-treatment. His appearance was so forbidding that one ship captain refused to accept him as a passenger. Fortunately the next one did.

Through all his misfortunes the Elephant Man had saved the card Treves had given him the day of their first meeting. The surgeon, he knew by instinct, was a man he could count on. And so, after many months, starving and exhausted, he had found himself looking up into Frederick Treves's kindly, worried face once more.

It was against the rules of the London Hospital, we have seen, to admit a patient suffering from a chronic disease. F. C. Carr Gomm, the hospital chairman, took every step he could to get the little man accepted by the hospitals that cared for the incurable. But none of them would have him—not even if all his expenses were paid.

The only place left for him to go was the workhouse. And poor Joseph, Carr Gomm reflected sadly, hated the workhouse worse than death.

Suddenly an idea flashed across the chairman's mind. The British public! If he could arouse the sympathy of the public, it might open its heart to Joseph—and its purse strings as well. So Carr Gomm sat down and penned a long letter to the editor of England's greatest newspaper, the *Times* of London. In it he gave a moving account of Joseph's condition and his tragic story.

"Terrible though his appearance is," Carr Gomm concluded,

"so terrible indeed that women and nervous persons fly in terror from the sight of him, and that he is debarred from seeking to earn his livelihood in any ordinary way, yet he is superior in intelligence, can read and write, is quiet, gentle, not to say even refined in his mind. He occupies his time in the hospital by making with his one available hand little cardboard models, which he sends to the matron, doctor, and those who have been kind to him. Through all the

The cardboard model of a church that Merrick made (probably with a nurse's help) as a gift for Madge Kendal, his patron.

miserable vicissitudes of his life he has carried about a painting of his mother. . . .

"It is a case of singular affliction brought about through no fault of himself; he can but hope for quiet and privacy during a life which Mr. Treves assures me is not likely to be long.

"Can any of your readers suggest to me some fitting place where he can be received? And then I feel sure that, when that is found, charitable people will come forward and enable me to provide him with such accommodation."

Carr Gomm's appeal touched many hearts. Envelopes containing money for Joseph's care poured in to the London Hospital. The hospital's managing committee was touched too; they decided that, in this one case, they could bend their rules.

Far from the busy life of the hospital, in the basement, two rooms were found and remodeled to provide the Elephant Man with a quiet, comfortable place to live. One was a bedroom–sitting room with a private exit to the hospital gardens, the other a bathroom; he needed frequent baths to be free of the odor that came from his strange skin. Soon the hospital staff was jokingly calling his apartment "The Elephant House."

Joseph, who had been homeless for years, had a home of his own at last. But he simply couldn't believe it would be permanent. It was too good to be true. He kept worrying: Where am I to be sent next?

When the hospital couldn't keep him any longer, he said to Treves one day, after some hesitation, couldn't he be sent to a lighthouse? He had never actually seen one but he had seen a picture and he'd never forgotten it. The lighthouse held a special attraction for him, and the surgeon understood it. "There at least," Treves wrote, "no one could open a door and peep in at him."

Or perhaps, he also asked, he could be sent to a blind asylum. He had read about homes for the blind and he liked the idea of living among people who wouldn't be able to see his disfigurement. "I fancy," wrote Treves, "there was a half-formed idea in his mind that he might be able to win the affection of a woman if only she were without eyes to see." Treves finally convinced him he had nothing to worry about; people had sent in enough money to take care of his needs as long as he lived.

How does a person pass his long days in a hospital, as Joseph had to?

He was a great reader of books and newspapers. He wrote letters. Madge Kendal, a leading actress, sent him a phonograph, and he loved to listen to it. She also provided money for basket-weaving lessons. Working slowly and carefully with his one good hand, he made many baskets, giving them to people who showed kindness to him. His first basket was a gift to the generous Mrs. Kendal. Another gift to her was a Gothic church he made of card-board.

Day by day Joseph appeared less frightened. He began to lose his haunted look. He came to know the hospital people who bustled about and he made friends with some. But he never dared to leave his rooms before night had fallen. Then, concealed beneath his hat and cloak, he left through his private exit and moved about the hospital grounds enjoying the fresh night air. When, as sometimes happened, some unfeeling wardmaid or porter opened his door to let curious friends peep in, he recoiled in anxiety and alarm.

If Joseph was to have any real happiness out of life, Treves realized, he needed to feel that people in general didn't view him as a monster. He looked up to women—and women in particular were frightened by his grotesque appearance. Wouldn't it help him if he learned they could treat him as a normal human being?

One day Treves persuaded a friend of his, an attractive young widow, to pay a visit to Joseph. All she would have to do, he told her, was smile at the disfigured man pleasantly, say good morning, and shake him by the hand.

The visit unleashed deep emotions in Joseph. After the pretty widow let go his hand he bent his head down over his knees and burst into tears. It was the first time, he told the surgeon, that a young woman had ever smiled at him and taken his hand.

"From this day," Treves wrote, "he began to change, little by little, from a hunted thing into a man. It was a wonderful change to witness and one that never ceased to fascinate me."

Carr Gomm's letter to the *Times* had aroused the sympathy of many socially prominent people, including members of the nobility, and numbers of them called on Joseph. Often they brought gifts such as flowers and pictures, and books, which he treasured most of all. In his situation another person might have been spoiled by these attentions or taken advantage of his visitors. But not Joseph; he remained the same humble, grateful person he had always been. As his shyness dropped from him he seemed less aware of how unsightly he was. For this Treves could take some credit; he would never allow any mirrors in the little man's rooms.

In the short life of Joseph Merrick, May 21, 1887, was the high-water mark. On that day Alexandra, Princess of Wales, visited the London Hospital to dedicate a new building. Her husband (later King Edward VII) came with her. After, the two went downstairs with Treves to call on the hospital's best-known patient. The princess gave Joseph a bouquet of flowers. Seating herself at his side, she spoke to him with warmth and friendliness, and the prince joked with him.

Later the princess sent Joseph a signed photograph of herself. He cried over it. It was a holy icon to him; he was hardly willing to let Treves touch it. The princess remembered the handicapped man with a card every Christmas and paid him more visits. The prince sent him grouse from his country estate. Joseph, only a short while earlier the lowliest of the lowly, was walking on clouds.*

*Merrick was not the only one to benefit from the royal visits. Treves became surgeon to the Prince and Princess of Wales and other members of the royal family, among them Queen Victoria and King George V. He was credited with saving the life of Edward VII by operating on him for appendicitis; he was made a baronet and given a lifelong residence on the royal estate at Richmond Park.

Many other ladies, learning the Princess of Wales had sent Joseph her photograph, imitated her example. The little man was thrilled. "His mantelpiece and table," wrote Treves, "became so covered with photographs of handsome ladies, with dainty knick-knacks and pretty trifles, that they may almost have befitted the apartment of an Adonis-like actor or of a famous tenor."

Of all the callers at "The Elephant House" Treves was the most faithful. He often visited his patients at the hospital on Sundays and stayed for long chats with the little man. Joseph now struck him as one of the most contented people he had ever known. More than once he heard him say, "I am happy every hour of the day."

Other men, Treves reflected, would have shown their contentment by singing or whistling. "Unfortunately poor Merrick's mouth was so deformed that he could neither whistle nor sing. . . . One thing that always struck me as sad about Merrick was the fact that he could not smile. Whatever his delight might be, his face remained expressionless. He could weep but he could not smile."

Joseph, Treves found, although a man in his twenties, had many of the qualities of a child. One of the most striking was his love of make-believe.

The little man's visitors sometimes left money with the surgeon to be spent on Joseph. One year, in early December, Treves asked his patient what he would like for Christmas.

Joseph eyed Treves shyly. Then he produced an illustrated advertisement and hesitantly held it out. It showed a leather dressing case with silver fittings and described the contents. Treves was astonished. What could the little man want with a dressing case?

It seemed ridiculous. The items in the case could serve no purpose for someone in Joseph's condition. He couldn't use the ivory-handled razor to shave his disfigured face. He had hardly any hair left to brush with the silver-backed brushes. He didn't need a silver shoehorn to put on his loose slippers. As for the cigarette case—why, his deformed lips couldn't close enough to hold a cigarette between them.

Joseph Merrick, dressed in his Sunday best, sits for the photographer. Note the enormous deformed right hand.

It took Treves a while to puzzle out why Joseph would want such a gift. The surgeon had two small daughters, and watching them probably helped. Just as a little girl playing she is a princess puts on a tinsel crown and pulls along a window curtain behind her for a train, Joseph needed the dressing case for a favorite fantasy of his own—making believe he was a fashionable man about town. A duke had given him a silver watch and chain for his vest; a lord had made him a present of a walking stick. Adding a dressing case to these, in his boyish imagination he could transform himself into the stylish young man of his dreams.

That Christmas Joseph got his dressing case. Every day he carefully set out on his table all the items in the case and sat admiring them. As he looked at them he was no longer a poor patient in the basement of the London Hospital; he was a smartly dressed clubman, a darling of the ladies, chatting with them gaily in some elegant London drawing room.

On one of Treves's visits Joseph told him that he had never been to the theater and he longed to go sometime.

You shall have your wish, my lad, the surgeon said to himself. But then he began to wonder: How can Joseph, in his incredible cap and cloak, walk into a theater without causing an uproar? That would be a hard nut to crack.

At Christmastime, with the help of the actress Madge Kendal, Treves obtained an entire private box at the Drury Lane Theatre, one of London's finest. Then, with three nurses in evening gowns, he drove Joseph to the theater in a coach with the curtains drawn. By arrangement, the coach stopped at the royal entrance and they smuggled the masked man up a private staircase. In the shadows at the rear of the box, shielded from public gaze by the nurses seated in front, Joseph watched a special holiday extravaganza, *Puss in Boots.* He was so awed and excited that he often panted for breath, just like a young child.

For a long time after, when Treves came to see him, Joseph kept talking about his evening at the theater. To him the play had not been make-believe; it was an event in real life that he had watched as though through a window, and he spoke of it as if it were still going on. "I wonder what the prince did after we left," he mused one day. And on another: "Mr. Treves, do you think that poor man is still in the dungeon?"

A deep, new longing stirred in Joseph's soul: to spend some time in the country. It was another hard nut to crack, but the surgeon cracked this one too. He arranged for Lady Louisa Knightley to let his patient stay in a gamekeeper's cottage on her estate near Northampton. Joseph was taken in a curtained carriage to a railroad siding, where, to his amazement, a special railroad coach was waiting. The coach, with blinds drawn and Joseph its only passenger, was shunted to the station and attached to the mainline train. He traveled by himself all the way to Northampton, where he was whisked by coach to the estate.

At the gamekeeper's cottage the poor little man's vacation almost ended before it had begun. No one had given the gamekeeper's wife a hint about her guest's appearance. The moment he took off his mask she gasped; overcome with fright, she threw her apron over her head and ran out of the house. But she soon calmed down, apologized, and treated him with kindness.

For six weeks Joseph had the time of his life. After being shut up so long in the hospital he could at last feel the sun on his face. He could wander about freely in the deep woods, without a cloak or cap—and without a worry that anyone would spy on him.

Joseph loved to write letters. Now he sent one after another to the surgeon. With the enthusiasm of a young boy he told about his exciting adventures in the country. He had met a frightening dog but had made friends with him. He had seen and heard birds that to him were strange and wonderful. He had watched trout shooting along a sparkling stream. He had accidentally startled a hare from its resting place—and been almost as startled himself. He had picked rare wildflowers (rare to him; to Treves they looked commonplace), which he pressed between the pages of his letters.

When Joseph got back to the hospital Treves found his health was much improved and he was happy to be "home" again. The following two summers the surgeon arranged for his patient to vacation in the country again.

Like most people of his time, Joseph had had a strong religious upbringing. Through all his many troubles his religion had been a great help to him. He regularly attended the services held in the hospital chapel. Naturally, his deformities made it impossible for him to sit in a pew and worship with the other patients. But the chaplain allowed him to stay in the vestry, with the door open just a crack; there he could hear the services and, unseen by anybody, take part in them.

Although Joseph always appeared cheerful, his physical problems never stopped increasing. His head had grown so big and heavy it was hard for him to hold it up. For years he had found it

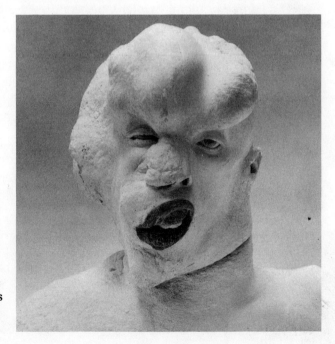

The deformities of Merrick's head are very striking in this plaster cast made after he died.

impossible to sleep lying down. If he tried, his massive head would sink deep into the pillows until the pressure on his neck made it difficult to breathe. He had no choice but to sleep sitting up in bed. With pillows propping him up in back, he would draw up his legs and, leaning forward, clasp his arms around them and rest his head on his knees.

On Easter Sunday, April 6, 1890, he attended two separate services, sitting in the vestry and praying. The chaplain gave him holy communion in private. The little man became deeply emotional. He told the chaplain he was very grateful for everything that had been done for him in the hospital. His voice shook as he declared it was the mercy of God to him that had brought him there.

He was suffering from bronchitis. Although he was only twenty-seven, he had a heart condition. Because of his increasing weakness, he normally spent the first part of the day in bed reading. He seldom got up before the afternoon.

On Thursday night, April 10, he went out by his private door and limped about in the hospital garden, enjoying the cool air.

On Friday morning, when his nurse came in to see to his needs, he appeared in his usual health. He was sitting up in bed when she left.

At 1:30 P.M. the wardmaid brought in his midday meal and set it on the table for him to eat when he wanted to. She thought he looked perfectly normal.

No one saw him again until after three, when Treves's house surgeon, Mr. Hodges, came in to check on the patient.

The first thing Hodges noticed was Joseph's food. It was untouched, just as the wardmaid had left it.

Hodges looked at Joseph. He was lying in an odd position, across the bed. He was very quiet.

Hodges could tell at a glance the little man was dead.

It was a shock, but they had always expected he would go like that: suddenly.

Hodges rushed out in search of Mr. Ashe, the senior surgeon, and brought him back. The two examined the body to determine the cause of death.

For three and a half years the deformed man had been the London Hospital's best-known patient.* The Prince and Princess of Wales as well as many of London's greatest celebrities had been his patrons. An inquest had to be held. Joseph's father, who had beaten him so savagely, did not attend; his uncle, who had taken him in when he ran away from home, did, and he identified the body. The jury accepted Mr. Ashe's verdict: death from asphyxia.

Treves did not testify. But long afterward, in a memoir he wrote about the Elephant Man, he told what he thought had happened.

Treves recalled that many times he had heard Joseph say that he wished he could lie down to sleep "like other people."

On that last day, the surgeon said, "he must, with some determination, have made the experiment. The pillow was soft, and the head, when placed on it, must have fallen backwards and caused a dislocation of the neck. Thus it came about that his death was due to the desire that had dominated his life—the pathetic but hopeless desire to be 'like other people.' "

Of all Treves's thousands of patients, the Elephant Man always remained the most special.

"He had passed through the fire and come out unscathed," the surgeon wrote. "His troubles had ennobled him. He showed himself to be a gentle, affectionate and lovable creature, as amiable as a happy woman, free from any trace of cynicism or resentment, without a grievance and without an unkind word for anyone. I have

He still is. Though dead almost a hundred years, Merrick has never left the London Hospital. In the museum of its medical college are exhibited his skeleton, casts of his arms, his right foot, and his head and shoulders. The museum also has the hat and mask he wore and the cardboard cathedral he made for Mrs. Kendal. In 1987 the singer Michael Jackson offered one million dollars for the skeleton. "The Board of Governors' decision," a museum official wrote the author, "is that as the skeleton is still of worldwide medical interest . . . it will not be sold."

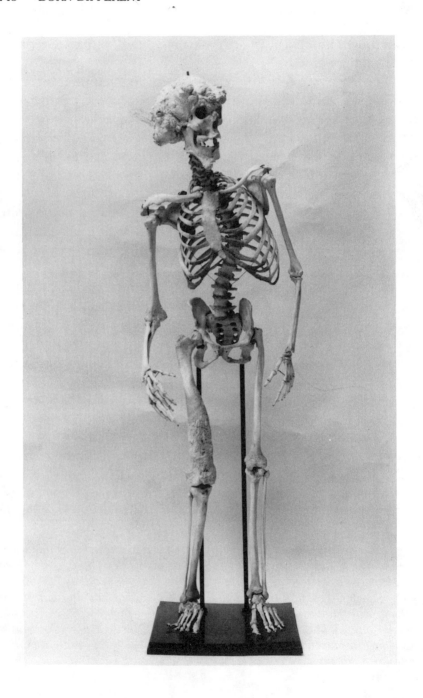

never heard him complain. I have never heard him deplore his ruined life. . . .

"As a specimen of humanity, Merrick was ignoble and repulsive; but the spirit of Merrick, if it could be seen in the form of the living, would assume the figure of an upstanding and heroic man, smooth browed and clean of limb, and with eyes that flashed undaunted courage."

Merrick's skeleton, with his other memorabilia, is preserved in the museum of the London Hospital Medical College. Note the curve in the spine and other abnormalities of the bones.

How to play a violin without hands: Herrmann Unthan at twenty, in 1867, when he first performed in Vienna.

The Armless Wonder

The birth was completely normal.

The baby was not.

The midwife was the first to notice. Shaking her head grimly, she wrapped the screaming infant in a blanket and hurried with him into the next room, where the new father, the village schoolmaster, was waiting anxiously.

Gottfried Unthan's face lit up. But when the woman opened the blanket to show him the naked child the smile froze on his lips.

From each of his newborn son's shoulders, in place of an arm, hung a stump about as long as a hand, and from each stump grew one tiny finger.

The father stood speechless.

Not the midwife. All that needed to be done, she said quietly, was to press a pillow down over his face. It would be over in an instant. Everybody would be better off.

The schoolmaster shook his head angrily. He informed her he wouldn't have a hand in anybody's murder—least of all his own son's.

The woman, who probably had hastened other deformed children on their way and been well rewarded for it, snorted her disapproval.

The baby was tucked inside the waiting crib. His mother, exhausted, was resting, and no one wanted to disturb her. She would learn the bad news soon enough.

After a time the mother stirred and asked for her child. The schoolmaster carried him to her. As gently as he could he told her their baby had been born without arms. Then he gave the sleeping child to her.

She opened the blanket and examined him all over. Her eyes shone with tears. "He is our son. God sent him to us and God will not forsake him." The baby had awakened and she put him to her breast. He sucked hungrily.

News of the birth of the boy without arms on April 5, 1848, spread rapidly from the small farming town of Sommerfeld, in East Prussia, Germany. When he was christened Carl Herrmann Unthan a few days later, for miles around people were talking about him. Many of them echoed the midwife. A child without arms! What need was there for such a one in a world where even a person with a good pair of arms had such a hard time making a go of it? What a tragedy for the poor parents!

Births like the Unthan boy's were rare but they weren't unknown. Babies were, and are, born without arms or without legs, or without any limbs at all, or with just vestiges of them. Today we call the condition a birth defect. Many babies who have one are born dead or die soon after birth.

What causes such a defect? Most commonly it's the result of a change in the genetic structure or a mutation. Our physical inheritance is determined by our genes—more than one hundred thousand of them—passed on to us by our parents. Sometimes a chemical change occurs in one or more of these genes. When this happens the child may be born with abnormal characteristics, as the Unthan boy was.

Medicines taken by the mother may also produce conditions like the Unthan baby's. Some years ago a drug called thalidomide was prescribed as a sedative for pregnant women before it had been adequately tested. Thousands of deformed children, some with only partial limbs, were born as a result. Thalidomide was promptly banned.*

With any baby, parents take care of all its needs. In the first year of life a child without arms may hardly miss them. Herrmann (as the Unthan baby was called) was an active, healthy child; except for his missing arms he was completely normal. His parents could take comfort at least in that.

One day, when the boy was about nine months old, his father was suddenly struck by the fact that little Herrmann reached out for things with his feet whenever they were bare. He was greatly impressed.

The schoolmaster called his wife and told her to look. *"Don't put any shoes or socks on the little rascal,"* he ordered.

After that, little Herrmann never wore shoes or socks except when his parents took him somewhere. The more he used his toes, feet, and legs, the stronger and more flexible they became. Soon he was pulling things toward himself with his feet and putting them in his mouth, snatching toys away from other children just the way they snatched his, and hitting back at them with his feet when they hit him with their hands.

Many times, when relatives or friends saw the armless little fellow, their hearts would melt with pity. Emotional ladies would cluck over him and moan, "Poor, poor child, what a terrible affliction! We'll pray to the Lord to call you to Him!" The boy didn't understand a word but he could see the pain on their faces and hear the distress in their voices. Suddenly he was sobbing as if he would never stop.

Gottfried Unthan wasn't slow to notice. A child who was constantly pitied, he realized, could soon learn to feel sorry for himself—and go on feeling sorry for himself as long as he lived. *"I don't want my son to be pitied by anybody!"* the schoolmaster cried

---

*Defective limbs may have other causes. These include a riboflavin (vitamin B_2) deficiency in the mother or an infection in her uterus.

whenever he saw people drowning Herrmann in their sympathy. Hearing the iron ring in his voice,they quickly obeyed.

It happened one evening at dinner, soon after his second birthday. Herrmann was seated next to his mother. Before feeding the armless boy, Mrs. Unthan held out a heaping bowl of porridge to his sister, on his other side. As the food passed the hungry little fellow he raised his leg and, reaching out his bare foot, scooped up some of the cereal with his toes and crammed it into his mouth. A smile of satisfaction spread over his cereal-smeared face. Everyone laughed.

"Wash the little rascal," his father ordered. "Give him a spoon and let him feed himself."

A spoon was placed between the boy's toes. His success with it was only moderate; as much food ended on the floor as in his mouth. Everyone reached out to help—except his father.

"Let the youngster do it his own way!" cried the schoolmaster. *"Anyone who tries to help him will answer to me."*

The old saying that practice makes perfect held true in Herrmann's case. Before very long he was eating and drinking by himself.

All through his childhood the boy heard these incidents related over and over again. They engraved themselves on his memory. The three commandments his father had laid down, Herrmann would write many years later, "made me an independent, able-bodied human being. I wonder if he was then aware that by his commandments he was laying the foundation of my future independence."

At three the boy decided it was high time he learned to wash himself. He pushed a chair over to the family washbasin and climbed up. Then, leaning against the back of the chair, he thrust one bare foot at a time into the water inside the basin. The floor was soon sopping wet but he was too busy to notice.

Mr. and Mrs. Unthan heard the splashing and came rushing in. Another father might have scolded the dripping boy, but not this one. "From now on, Herrmann must wash himself," he said.

It took some coaching and much care—but before long the boy was doing almost as neat and thorough a job as his older brother and sister.

Herrmann was only four when he started to teach himself to read and write. In little rural Sommerfeld the school was no more than a large room in the rickety old farmhouse where the schoolmaster and his family made their home. One day, perhaps drawn by the voices of the children chanting their ABC's, the boy crept over to the classroom door. Pushing it open quietly, he slipped inside and hid under a table.

It was easy to get a slate and a piece of chalk. Holding the chalk in his right foot, between the big toe and its neighbor, he painstakingly scratched out the letters his father was writing on the blackboard. Day after day he came back to study by himself under the table. Nobody ever noticed the silent scholar.

When Herrmann turned six, he was officially enrolled in the one-room school. No one could have been more astonished than the schoolmaster when he saw that his armless son already had a good grasp of the essentials of reading and writing. He had the village carpenter build a special desk for the boy, one that would be low enough, so he wouldn't have any trouble resting his legs on it and writing with his foot. By his second year in school he was so far ahead in his studies that his father assigned him to help beginners.

Singing lessons were a regular part of the schoolwork. These were Herrmann's particular joy. The assistant teacher wrote the notes of the music on the blackboard for the pupils to follow, but many either never learned to read them or found the songs too hard to sing. Not so the armless boy. He had a fine ear for music; he could sing the most difficult melodies the instant he laid eyes on the notes.

For someone who has no arms, putting on clothes and taking them off can be full of problems. Herrmann's mother always

Paris Nov. 23ᵈ 1893

Messrs. Koster, Bial & Cᵒ. New York.

Gentlemen

I received both your cable & letter, containing contract & I must say that you show such a considerable amount of "enterprising pluck" as to astonish me to perplexity.

My performance has been seen here & in London by J.S. Cooney, John D. Hopkins & various other American Managers, & every one of them was afraid to introduce me in the U.S. "for fear of feet", so that I had come to the conclusion those useful lower members must have been rather neglected by the U.S Public, to cause such an animosity. — Well, I shall come & see myself, & I trust that I'll do like Cesar: vene, vidi, vici. I wish & hope that the New York. Public will reward your courage & flock in by thousends to see my act. you fully deserve it!

Most faithfully yours

C. H. Unthan

This letter, written by Unthan with his foot, is more legible than many written by hand. He was also an excellent typist.

dressed and undressed him. One night when she went into his room to help him take off his clothes he was already under the blankets. Over the back of the chair next to his bed lay his clothing, all neatly folded.

"Who took your clothes off for you?" she asked in surprise.

"I undressed all by myself."

She called his father in. Neither of them could believe him. They wanted proof. Telling him to get out of bed, his mother dressed him in his trousers and jacket. Then they asked him to show them how he had taken his clothes off and folded them away so neatly.

The boy was only too eager to oblige. He seated himself on the chair. Raising his right foot, he grasped the front of his jacket with his versatile toes and tugged and tugged until his astonished parents saw him pull it up over his head and off.

His trousers came next. To open the buttons he took a deep breath and pulled in his stomach. Then he thrust the toes of his right foot between the buttons and undid them one at a time. Standing up, he shook himself; the trousers fell to the floor. Finally he picked up the garments with his foot and folded them neatly over the back of the chair. His mother and father, hugging him, heard the boy promise that next he was going to tackle the much harder job of dressing all by himself. He proved as good as his word.

Young children love to help with simple household chores. To a handicapped child, doing these little tasks often means much more than it can to a normal one: it gives him a very special sense of achievement. One day Herrmann came upon a pair of his father's shoes and saw they were crusted with mud. These need cleaning! he said to himself. Getting a cloth, he laboriously rubbed the mud off, then gave the shoes a shine. After that, polishing the family's shoes became one of the boy's regular chores. So did going to a nearby village to buy fresh fish, which he carried home in a basket hung from his neck.

Besides his older brother and sister, the armless child had a younger brother named Robert. Herrmann loved little Robert and often sang him to sleep when he was a baby. One winter Robert took sick. He had great difficulty breathing and there was a terrible rattle in his throat. After a few days he died.

Herrmann was given the heartbreaking job of inviting people to the funeral. When the day came, the schoolmaster's house was full. People went up to the coffin and looked at the rosy-cheeked little boy inside. Sitting nearby, Herrmann could not help hearing several of them say, "Again the good Lord has taken the wrong one!" He wished he had died in his brother's place.

Herrmann's father had a farm he worked when he wasn't teaching school. Along with his older brother and sister, the armless boy used to help in the fields. When the cows and horse needed to be watered it was Herrmann who led them to the pond. After the grass was mowed he swept it together and piled it up with his feet. Potatoes were an important crop. Little Herrmann followed behind the plow and thrust manure into the newly opened furrows with one foot while he supported his weight on the other. When the potatoes were ripe he dug down into the soil with his toes and lifted the tubers out. He became so fast that he could do two rows in the time it took his brother and sister to do one.

More than once, when the boy was learning these jobs, his feet got bruised and bloody and his legs extremely tired. But as he worked his skin grew tough and his feet and legs enormously powerful and supple; in time he could swing them and twist them and use them in ways no ordinary human being could. His brother and sister sometimes grumbled about having to labor in the fields under the hot sun. But Herrmann didn't mind. For him it wasn't work so much as exciting, rewarding fun; it left him feeling tired but good, the way a strenuous game did. He had no arms—but he could be useful!

By the time Herrmann reached ten he'd learned just about all he could in the little country school. He gave more and more of his time to helping in the classroom. The schoolmaster could see his little armless rascal deserved a better future than the small farming village could offer. In front of the boy, one day, he placed a Latin grammar. Latin was a hard language, but anyone who wanted a higher education in those times had to know it. The child buried his nose in the book, studying it with the same eagerness with which he had mastered reading and writing.

Not long after, a small and seemingly insignificant thing happened that was to change his life forever.

The assistant teacher, Fritz, sometimes played his violin for the schoolchildren. Eyes shining, the armless boy watched entranced. Each movement Fritz made, each sound he drew from the instrument, thrilled him. With his fine ear and his love of music, he wanted nothing in the world so much as to play the violin.

One night at dinner he got up his nerve and asked his father for violin lessons.

Everyone at the table burst into laughter. How in heaven's name could a child play the violin without arms?

Herrmann could barely control his fury. He ran from the table in tears. When he finally calmed down he came to a decision: if he couldn't have violin lessons he would teach himself.

After school one day, when no one was about, Herrmann quietly borrowed Fritz's violin and bow, carried them* into his room, and bolted the door. Instantly he was confronted by a problem. To play a violin you have to hold it—and he had no arms. He tried gripping it under his chin. No good. He laid it on the floor. In this position, holding the bow with his toes, he could play only one string. He turned the violin this way and that. Nothing worked.

Tears flooded his eyes. His family had been right after all!

The violin was resting on the floor. He sat and looked at its shining, graceful shape and his heart ached. Then he told himself:

*To carry large objects he gripped them securely between his chin and collarbone. For smaller things he used his mouth, as will be explained later.

There has to be a way. I won't give up.

When the idea came to him it seemed too simple. He couldn't believe it would work. But he got a piece of cord and carefully fastened the instrument on top of a low stool. Next he sat down on his chair in front of it and raised his legs. The toes of his right foot came to rest on the strings and pressed down gently. The toes of his left foot lifted the bow and drew it experimentally across the strings.

It wasn't music. It was noise. It grated on his ears. It sounded as if someone had imprisoned a crow inside the violin and the bird was cawing to be let out.

His forehead crinkled in concentration. His right foot toed the strings the way he'd seen Fritz finger them. The bow moved back and forth. He changed its angle, and he kept changing it.

Once in a long while—as if by a miracle—a tone that almost sounded musical came from the violin. There was hope!

Every day, as soon as school was out, he would borrow Fritz's violin and music book and lock himself in his room. He knew how to read music from his singing lessons and, opening the book, he tried to play a tune. He worked at it patiently. He invented new bow and fingering techniques with his flexible legs and toes. Week after week, month after month he worked, till he felt his legs were almost ready to fall off. Sometimes it seemed to him the crow had escaped from the violin and a songbird had taken its place. He never played without carefully bolting his door; the sound of his family's laughter when he said he wanted to play the violin still echoed in his mind.

One evening, as the boy was practicing, there was a loud rap on the door. His heart in his mouth, he opened up.

Gottfried Unthan walked in. He looked hard at the violin tied down to the stool and at his son's worried face. "Play," he said.

His foot shaking, Herrmann lifted the bow. The instant it touched the strings the violin seemed to play by itself. He forgot anyone was in the room with him; all he was aware of was the music. How much he loved it!

When Herrmann stopped he saw his father's mouth was curved in a smile. "I shall ask Freitag [the village music teacher] to give you lessons." Tears welled up in the boy's eyes.

Money was never too plentiful in the Unthan household. But somehow the schoolmaster scraped up enough to buy Herrmann a violin of his own. His mother sewed a bag of leather to protect it. Carrying it slung over his shoulder, the armless boy walked through the village streets, his head held very high, to the home of his violin teacher.

By the time Herrmann turned fifteen he had learned as much as he could from a country music teacher, and his father sent him to Königsberg, a nearby city, for advanced training and general studies. The violin was the boy's life; he worked at it day and night. In his spare time he visited the institute for the blind, where he helped sightless children with their music studies. In his own studies he forged ahead so far and so fast that his excited parents began to hope he might one day become a professional violinist. After a year they sent him to the great city of Leipzig for lessons at its famed high school of music.

For the sixteen-year-old from the country the Leipzig school was a complicated, dizzying world. There were classes in aesthetics, the history of music, and other new subjects. And all around there were unfamiliar, unsmiling faces. His fellow students at first showed enormous curiosity about the strange bird that had joined their flock. They watched in astonishment the first time he played for them. Immediately afterward they pounced on him, snobbishly finding one fault after another with his playing. Their biting remarks set his face on fire.

In other places Herrmann had found the students would keep their distance from him; they seemed to pretend he wasn't there. It had hurt, but with time he had taught himself to take no notice. At the high school, however, the pain he'd felt in the past he began to feel again, as if a half-healed wound had started to bleed once more. He had never been so far from home before. He was an adolescent now, with the drives, the self-doubts, the need for companionship every adolescent feels. Shunned by his classmates, he felt terribly alone until he discovered another outsider at the school, a boy from America. Their loneliness drew the two together and they became fast friends.

Study and practice. Practice and study. Herrmann's playing got better all the time. A high point of his years in Leipzig came when one of his professors invited him to play a solo piece at a charity concert. The professor also offered the boy the use of his own violin, the work of a master craftsman, a rare Guarneri more than a hundred years old. Not many young violinists ever have the good fortune to play a Guarneri or even to touch one. A shiver of awe flashed through the boy's body the first time he ran the bow across its strings.

The night of the charity concert arrived. The hall was sold out. Stepping out on the platform and looking at the upturned faces, Herrmann was surprised that he felt no stage fright; somehow he was strangely calm.

After bowing, he sat down in front of the stool holding the violin and slipped his feet out of his shoes. Whenever he played in public he wore socks whose front part had been cut off, leaving his feet half bare. He began to tune the instrument with his toes. At the unusual sight exclamations of wonder rippled through the audience. They died down as the Guarneri began to sing under his toes.

When Herrmann finally laid down his bow he heard not a sound, not a single handclap. Disappointed, he started to walk off the stage. An instant later a cloudburst of applause swept through the hall. The audience refused to stop clapping until he came back and gave them an encore. Then the storm of applause started again. It must have been the incredible Guarneri, Herrmann said to himself.

Next morning the newspapers printed reviews of the concert. The boy's heart leaped as he read praise of his performance and of the imaginative ways he had used his toes to make up for the fingers he had been denied.

As he read on, the blood turned to ice in his veins. After praising him, most of the critics expressed strong doubts that he had any future as a violinist. The demands of the concert stage were stern, they declared; an armless fiddler could never hope to satisfy them.

And he had been stupid enough to think he could make a life for himself in music! It was for this his parents had scrimped and saved and sacrificed for so long!

Of his nineteen years he had already devoted nine to the violin. His teachers had told him they had given him everything they could; the rest was up to him. Good violin technique demanded endless study and practice. But what was the point of more grueling work if his dream of a career on the concert stage was hopeless?

He had never felt such despair before in his life.

He tried to fight it. Perhaps there was something else he could do with his training. He could lower his sights. Suppose he tried to find a position as a member of an orchestra. Then he thought: What conductor would put up with a violinist who couldn't even set up his own music stand?

Suppose he lowered his sights still further. Maybe he could make some kind of a living teaching music to children. But that route, he saw at once, was closed to him too. No parent in his right mind would be willing to hire a violin teacher with no arms.

No, he would have to find some other means of earning a livelihood. What that might be, however, he couldn't imagine. When an invitation came from a conductor in Dresden to play at a few concerts there, he was able to thrust these worries out of his mind. But like vultures relentlessly following a stricken animal, they came back to haunt him as soon as he returned to Leipzig.

Shortly after, an elegantly dressed gentleman knocked at the door of Herrmann's boardinghouse. He said he was a theatrical agent looking for new talent; he had read about Herrmann's performances and wondered if he could hear him play. As the violinist's toes reached for his bow the visitor's eyes brightened with interest. When Herrmann finally set the bow down the agent told him he liked what he had seen and heard and he wanted to offer him a contract for a tour.

The boy could hardly believe his ears. In spite of the opinions of Leipzig's foremost critics, the gates of the world of music were swinging open to him after all!

Herrmann's tour began in Würzburg, in southern Germany, where he played to crowded houses. Then he and his agent moved on to the metropolis of Frankfurt. Here he was part of a variety or vaudeville show—one of a number of entertainers. At his first performance he had a piece of bad luck. Just as he was starting to play, one of his violin strings broke. Gasps of sympathy rose from the audience.

Undisturbed, Herrmann reached his toes toward a box of strings he kept in his violin case. Fishing one out, he fastened it in the place of the broken one. Then he shut the violin case. This made a noise as loud as a rifle shot, and laughter exploded through the theater.

Herrmann, tuning his instrument, had trouble hearing how it sounded. Putting his big toe to his mouth, he said, *"Shhh!"*

The audience had never seen anything so comical before. It howled its amusement. After that, everything he played was received with hearty applause.

In Munich the audience loved his performance. With his agent he crossed the Austrian border; he was booked to appear in one of the best halls in Vienna, one that featured the great conductor Johann Strauss. Popular demand kept him in the city for a month.

In the newspapers and magazines enthusiastic articles appeared about the armless violinist, some illustrated with caricatures. Earlier, seeing himself and the way he played pictured so humorously might have caused him sharp pain; now, however, everything was different. Flushed with success, he could throw back his head and laugh. In spite of his handicap—in fact, partly because of it—he would be able to make his own way in the world. He would never again need anything from his mother and father but their love. And he could start to pay them back for all they had done for him.

The young fiddler's tour took him to Budapest. Once, in the front row of the crowded auditorium, he saw a face that made him start in disbelief. Franz Liszt, the famous composer, the greatest pianist of the age, had come to hear him play! When the concert ended Liszt came up and praised his performance.

After endless miles of travel Herrmann found himself in the capital of Russia, St. Petersburg, with its onion-domed cathedrals and splendid palaces. He had just finished a performance when he saw a stern-faced man in uniform snooping about backstage. The man came up to him and, in a voice that rang with authority, began to question him.

How, he demanded suspiciously, had Herrmann produced his music?

The violinist was puzzled.

"I am the chief of police," the officer growled. He quickly made clear that he believed Herrmann was a fraud and the music that seemed to come from his violin was played by a fiddler tucked away backstage.

The musician invited the officer into his dressing room. Seating himself in front of his violin, he slipped off his shoes and took up the bow. The instant the first majestic notes reached the officer's ears he sprang to his feet. He snatched off his cap and his heels clicked together. When the music died away, he thanked Herrmann, saluted, and left. The chief had just heard a moving performance of the Russian national anthem and the young German from then on was a very welcome guest in the city.

It was a year before Herrmann's tour brought him back to Germany. Bookings were so heavy his agent wouldn't even allow him time off to visit his parents. In the train, on shipboard, in hotels at night he never stopped practicing. Before he arrived in each new country he taught himself its favorite melodies. He studied too, especially the languages of the countries he visited. In time he mastered seven.

Having played all over Europe, the armless violinist set out for the New World. He toured the United States and Cuba. Next came Mexico.

A London poster advertises some of the remarkable things Unthan had taught himself to do without hands. His achievements won him an international reputation.

Mexico in 1875 was torn by revolution. Railroad travel—where there were railroads—was unreliable, and so was travel by coach. The group of entertainers to which the violinist belonged were told they would have to cover great distances on horseback. Herrmann was an exception; he could ride in the wagon that was to follow them. But being the kind of man he was, he insisted on getting his own horse and riding with the rest.

How can a man without arms control a horse—make it start, stop, go slow, canter, gallop, turn left, turn right? The young violinist tackled these problems with the same inventive flare and patience he tackled everything else.

For some hours Herrmann watched his fellow entertainers learning to ride. Then he asked for a short strap of soft leather with a buckle at one end, and also for a length of string.

Taking the strap, the young man buckled it about his neck. Next he fastened the horse's reins to the strap with the string tied in a slipknot. (The thin string, he figured, would break if he tumbled out of the saddle and he would be free.) In ordinary riding, the reins hung on his chest by the string. When he wanted to guide or check the horse he bent his head, caught the reins between his teeth, and tugged on them. Pressing against the animal's flanks with his thighs gave further control. So did speaking to the horse in soft, soothing tones and making friends with him.

The armless violinist journeyed hundreds of miles on horseback, across difficult country pockmarked with rabbit holes and plagued by bandits and hostile Indians. More than once he fell from his mount or with him. Neither was ever hurt. After Mexico he toured the great cities of South America. He was to come back to the New World several times.

Over the years Herrmann kept adding to his skills. He became an expert marksman. Audiences watched openmouthed as he sat down in a chair at one end of the stage and picked up a rifle. A playing card, the ace of hearts, was held up by an assistant at the opposite end of the stage. Resting the rifle stock on his chest, the

The Armless Wonder was an expert shot. The emperor of Germany kept as a souvenir a pencil Unthan had shot in half.

butt against his chin, he supported the barrel end with the toes of his left foot and took aim. With one of the toes of his right foot he pulled the trigger. The bullet passed through the heart on the card.

He mastered the cornet and played it for his audiences. He typed for them too. With the typewriter on a stool before him, he seated himself and picked up two pencils. Holding each at the rubber end between the toes of each foot, he rapidly tapped out a short message without looking at the keyboard. Seven sheets of paper, with carbons, had already been inserted in the machine. Pulling the typewritten sheets out, he signed them with a pencil. Then he had the sheets handed out to people in the audience, who sometimes almost came to blows in their eagerness to get them.

But these were only a few of the remarkable things this remarkable man did. He would pick up a deck of cards, shuffle them, and deal them out to an assistant and himself. He did card tricks that never failed to mystify his audiences. In one part of his act he demonstrated comically how well he could entertain guests. Taking a bottle of wine, he uncorked it and poured it into glasses. A cake was set on the table and, picking up a knife with his toes, he cut it into perfectly matched portions.

Swimming might seem impossible for a man without arms. Not for this one, however. As a boy in East Prussia he had gone to a pond where he saw other boys swimming. Filling his chest with air and leaning over backward on the water, he slowly raised his feet and began to kick. The air in his lungs gave him buoyancy—and, as he expressed it, he had no arms to add to his weight and pull him down. By vigorous, regular kicking he found he could actually move across the water. Constant practice turned him into a powerful swimmer, and at fifteen he actually rescued a drowning man.

When he performed in circuses, he included swimming and diving in his act. An assistant would toss a coin and a plate into the water. The armless man then dove in. A moment or two later he would bob to the surface and open his mouth. The coin was inside. He held up his foot and between his toes was the plate.

Unthan was not only famous as a performer; he was well known in scientific circles for the extraordinary development of his feet and legs. He attracted the attention of one of the most important scientists in German medical history, Rudolf Virchow.* At a meeting of more than five hundred scholars and medical men in Berlin, Virchow asked the armless fiddler to give a demonstration of his skill. The audience was especially impressed by Unthan's ability to turn his thighs in the joints of the hips even beyond the degree that contortionists could, and also by how much he could spread out his toes and bend them.

*Rudolf Virchow (1821–1902) is celebrated as the father of modern pathology, or the study of diseases, but he also made contributions to almost every other branch of medicine, as well as to anthropology.

Aside from being armless, the violinist was normal in every respect. This included an interest in girls. As a young man he fell in love with the daughter of one of his managers. Although she returned his affection the romance came to a bitter end; her father wouldn't allow her to marry him because of his handicap.

Some years later, in Prague, Herrmann met a pretty young singer, Antonie Beschta. Her mother welcomed him when he came to call. Antonie's older sister sang too and played the piano, and when Herrmann proposed that they form a trio the girls liked the idea. So did the public, and for a good while the three entertainers traveled from country to country, giving concert performances. On Christmas Eve 1883, while staying with the Beschtas in Prague, Herrmann slipped out with Antonie for a few hours. When they returned a wedding ring glittered on her finger. It was the start of a long and happy life together.

A celebrity like Unthan met kings and queens and many other important and distinguished people. One person he never forgot was John D. Rockefeller, founder of the Standard Oil Company and one of the richest men in the world. The armless violinist was invited to dinner by a group of financial tycoons, including Rockefeller, in New York City. They watched with considerable curiosity as he buttered his bread, cut his meat, and drank. Afterward they pelted him with questions.

Rockefeller told Herrmann he was the happiest man he had ever met.

The violinist was surprised. "And what about you, with all your money, Mr. Rockefeller?" he asked.

"I can't buy your *joie de vivre* [zest for life]," the multimillionaire replied. "My money makes me a slave among slaves."

On a trip across the Atlantic Unthan struck up a friendship with a famous German writer named Gerhart Hauptmann. The armless man left such an impression on Hauptmann that he made him a character in a novel. In 1913 Unthan played himself in a motion picture based on the book. Later he was starred in another movie,

Even an armless man has to eat.

The Man Without Arms. A highlight of the film was to be a scene in which he rescued the drowning heroine. During rehearsals the scenario came true: the actress panicked and actually began to drown. Unthan, swimming on his back, pulled her to shore, gripping the neck of her blouse between his teeth and kicking vigorously.

Now and then we read about the large sums for which pianists insure their hands and singers their voices. Such an insurance policy would have come in very handy for Unthan, since from time to time he was the victim of an accident. Once, in London, a cab knocked him down and ran over his right leg. He was in bed for five weeks. When his agent came to him with an attractive offer for a booking in Madrid he had to sign the contract with his pen held between his teeth.*

In Munich, another time, he dislocated the big toe of his right foot and had to keep an ice bag on it for weeks. While he was recuperating he rewrote his music so he could play it without the injured toe, and went onstage before he was completely recovered.

When World War I started in 1914 Unthan was sixty-six. He was eager to help his country and he knew just how: by showing service-men who had lost limbs in battle that they could do more than they imagined with what they had left. Without receiving any pay he traveled from hospital to hospital, lecturing and giving demonstra-tions to amputees. (The emperor of Germany, Wilhelm II, who had a withered arm, saw a demonstration in Dresden and became one of Unthan's admirers.) He also wrote an inspiring book for service-men, illustrated with pictures of his feats. After the war the German government awarded him two decorations and a sum of money.

Unthan didn't retire until he was in his seventies. He still kept active, working as a reviewer of theatrical performances, tapping out his manuscripts with two pencils on his typewriter. On his eightieth birthday, in 1928, a leading circus in Berlin gave a benefit performance in the old trouper's honor, and hundreds of con-gratulatory telegrams, letters, and gifts poured into his home.

Unthan died in Berlin in 1929. A few years earlier he had published an autobiography in which he told the story of his handi-cap and his lifelong struggle to overcome it. Because he wrote the book with his feet, in contrast to a manuscript, which is written by hand, he titled it, with his unfailing sense of humor, "The Pediscript"

Unthan's mouth often had to substitute for his nonexistent hands. To pick up small objects like letters he drew his lips in over his teeth and, with the dry outer lips, picked up the objects. He moved chessmen and turned the pages of books in the same way. To judge the quality of cloth, he felt it between his upper lip and tongue.

(*Das Pediskript,* 1925).

At the start of his book the man with no arms set his favorite motto. He had learned it at his father's knee; it had guided him through all his days. A motto? Yes, but it was a battle cry too, and he wanted to shout it to anyone who had to struggle through life with a severe handicap, as he had:

WHERE THERE'S A WILL THERE'S A WAY

Selected Bibliography

Albon, Joan. *Little People in America: The Social Dimensions of Dwarfism.* New York: Praeger, 1984.

Barnum, P. T. *Struggles and Triumphs.* New York: Macmillan Company, 1936.

Bergsma, Daniel, M.D., ed. *Conjoined Twins.* New York: The National Foundation–March of Dimes, 1966.

Desmond, Alice C. *Barnum Presents General Tom Thumb.* New York: Macmillan Company, 1954.

Drimmer, Frederick. *The Elephant Man.* New York: G. P. Putnam's Sons, 1985.

———. *Very Special People: The Struggles, Loves, and Triumphs of Human Oddities.* Revised edition. New York: Bell Publishing Company, 1985.

Durant, John and Alice. *Pictorial History of the American Circus.* New York: A. S. Barnes and Company, 1957.

Fadner, Frederic. *The Gentleman Giant: Biography of Robert Pershing Wadlow.* Boston: Bruce Humphries, 1944.

Fitzsimons, Raymund. *Barnum in London.* New York: St. Martin's Press, 1970.

Howell, Michael, and Ford, Peter. *The True History of the Elephant Man.* Revised and illustrated edition. New York: Allison & Busby, 1983.

Hunter, Kay. *Duet for a Lifetime.* New York: Coward-McCann, 1964.

Treves, Sir Frederick. *The Elephant Man and Other Reminiscences.* London: Cassell & Company, 1923.

Twain, Mark. "Personal Habits of the Siamese Twins." In *Sketches New and Old.* New York: Harper & Brothers, 1903.

Unthan, Carl H. *The Armless Fiddler.* London: Allen and Unwin, 1935.

Wallace, Irving. *The Fabulous Showman: The Life and Times of P. T. Barnum.* New York: Alfred A. Knopf, 1959.

Wallace, Irving and Amy. *The Two: The Story of the Original Siamese Twins.* New York: Simon and Schuster, 1978.

Warkany, Josef, M.D. *Congenital Malformations.* Chicago: Year Book Medical Publishers, 1971.

Index